Tenth Edition

THE ARIZONA NOTARY LAW PRIMER

All the hard-to-find information every Arizona Notary Public needs to know!

National Notary Association

Published by

National Notary Association
9350 De Soto Ave.
Chatsworth, CA 91311-4926
(818) 739-4000
Fax: (818) 700-0920
Website: www.NationalNotary.org
Email: nna@nationalnotary.org

Copyright © 2011 National Notary Association
ALL RIGHTS RESERVED. No part of this book may be reproduced in
any form without permission in writing from the publisher.

The information in this *Primer* is correct and current at the time
of its publication, although new laws, regulations and rulings may
subsequently affect the validity of certain sections. This information
is provided to aid comprehension of state Notary Public requirements
and should not be construed as legal advice. Please consult an
attorney for inquiries relating to legal matters.

Tenth Edition, Third Printing
First Edition © 1993

ISBN: 978-1-59767-090-6
L.C. Control Number: 2005920442

Table of Contents

Introduction 1

How to Become an Arizona Notary 3

Tools of the Trade. 7

10 Most-Asked Questions. 10

Steps to Proper Notarization. 15

Notary Laws Explained 21
    The Notary Commission 21
    Official Notarial Acts. 28
    Practices and Procedures. 41
    Misconduct, Fines and Penalties .71

Test Your Knowledge 80

Arizona Laws Pertaining to Notaries Public. 86
    Arizona Revised Statutes 86
    Arizona Administrative Code 118
    Attorney General Opinions 124

Office of the Arizona Secretary of State. 125

Bureaus of Vital Statistics. 126

Hague Convention Nations 131

About the NNA 134

Index 136

For the latest updates on state laws
and requirements, please visit

NationalNotary.org/Primer-Updates

Have a Tough Notary Question?

If you were an NNA member, you could get the answer to that difficult question. Join the NNA and your membership includes access to the Notary Hotline* and live Notary experts providing the latest Notary information regarding laws, rules and regulations.

Hours
Monday – Friday   5:00 a.m. – 7:00 p.m. (PT)
Saturdays   5:00 a.m. – 5:00 p.m. (PT)

Hotline Toll-Free Phone Number: 1-888-876-0827

After hours you can leave a message or email our experts at Hotline@NationalNotary.org and they will respond the next business day.

*Access to the Notary Hotline is for NNA members only. Call and become a member today.

Introduction

You are to be commended on your interest in Arizona Notary law! Purchasing *The Arizona Notary Law Primer* identifies you as a conscientious professional who takes your official responsibilities seriously.

In few fields is the expression "more to it than meets the eye" more true than in Notary law. What often appears on the surface to be a simple procedure may, in fact, have important legal considerations. *The Arizona Notary Law Primer* is a resource created to help you decipher the state laws that affect notarization as well as to acquaint you with prudent Notary practices in general.

This edition of *The Arizona Notary Law Primer* has been updated to include the recent law changes. As of July 20, 2011, Notaries and electronic Notaries must be able to read and write English in order to qualify for a commission to perform notarial acts. Document signers must sign documents in a language a Notary understands. Document signers also must either be able to communicate directly with the Notary in the same language, or indirectly through a translator who is also present and who can communicate directly with the signer and the Notary in languages the translator understands. Notarial certificates must be worded and completed using only letters, characters, and a language read, written and understood by the Notary. If a certificate is attached to a document without notarial wording, the certificate must contain specific information to describe the document. Statute now explicitly authorizes a Notary to notarize a "translator's declaration," further clarifies that a Notary may not advertise a fee except as authorized by administrative rule, and presents additional scenarios in which a Notary would have a conflict of interest that would disqualify the Notary from notarizing.

ARIZONA NOTARY LAW PRIMER

While *The Arizona Notary Law Primer* begins with informative chapters on how to become a Notary Public, what tools a Notary needs, often-asked questions and critical steps in notarization, the heart of the book is the chapter titled "Notary Laws Explained." Here, we take you through Arizona's Notary laws and put them in easy-to-understand terms. Every pertinent section of the statutes is analyzed and explained, as are topics not covered by Arizona law but nonetheless of vital concern to you as a Notary Public.

For handy reference, we have reprinted the complete text of the laws of Arizona that relate to Notaries Public. In addition, we have included addresses and phone numbers of the Secretary of State's office and Bureaus of Vital Statistics for all U.S. states and jurisdictions. Finally, we have compiled a list of nations that are parties to the Hague Convention, a treaty which simplifies the process of authenticating notarized documents.

Whether you're about to be commissioned for the first time or are a longtime Notary, we're sure that *The Arizona Notary Law Primer* will provide you with new insight and understanding of your official duties. Your improved comprehension of Arizona's Notary law will naturally result in greater competence as a professional Notary Public.

> Milton G. Valera
> Chairman
> National Notary Association

How to Become an Arizona Notary Public

1. Ensure that you comply with the basic qualifications for an Arizona Notary commission.

First, you must be at least 18 years of age. Second, you must be a citizen or legal permanent resident of the United States. Third, you must be a resident of the state of Arizona for income tax purposes and claim your residence in the state as your primary residence on state and federal tax returns. Fourth, you must not be a convicted felon, unless your civil rights have been restored. Fifth, you must be able to read and write English.

There is no minimum time of state residency required — you can apply for a commission on the same day you enter Arizona. A "legal resident of Arizona" is a person who is residing in the state and who intends to stay, usually indicated by taking action to obtain a driver's license, registering to vote or the like.

Your civil rights must not currently be revoked as a result of a felony conviction or other judicial proceeding. You may apply to become a Notary with a previous conviction, provided your civil rights have been restored and you supply a copy of the court papers that restore your civil rights with your application. Even if your civil rights have been restored, however, the Secretary of State may deny your application if the conviction pertains to the duties of a Notary Public.

Every Arizona Notary is required to keep a reference manual that describes the duties, authority and ethical responsibilities of Notaries. You may download the current version of the *Arizona Notary Public Reference Manual* from the Secretary of State's website (www.azsos.gov), or request a manual by phone

(602-542-4758), email (notary@azsos.gov) or regular mail from the Secretary of State's office at the following address:

> Arizona Secretary of State
> Attention: Notary Section
> 1700 W. Washington Street, 7th Floor
> Phoenix, AZ 85007-2888

The Arizona Secretary of State may require applicants for a Notary commission to attend a training course before receiving their commissions. The Secretary may also require renewing Notaries to attend a training course within the ninety days preceding renewal of their commissions.

2. Obtain a commission application.

You may obtain the official application for an Arizona Notary commission from the Secretary of State's office in one of three ways:

(1.) by downloading it online at http://www.azsos.gov/business_Services/Forms/Notary/Application.pdf

(2.) by calling 602-542-4758 and requesting that an application be mailed or faxed to you, or

(3.) by requesting a form in person at the Secretary of State's office.

If you are renewing your current Notary commission, you must go through the same process as when applying for a first-time commission. The Secretary of State will send you a renewal notice and application 60 to 90 days before your current commission expires. If you do not receive a renewal notice, contact the Secretary of State's office.

3. Complete the application form.

Carefully follow the instructions, and completely fill in all the blanks on the form, whether you are applying online or on paper. Leave the box in the upper right of the paper application empty, however. Any information in that box is for office use only. If you are filling out a paper form, make sure you type or print neatly in ink. The Secretary of State will return any application that is unreadable, thus delaying the start of your commission.

HOW TO BECOME AN ARIZONA NOTARY PUBLIC

Fill in your name exactly how you want your Notary commission to be issued, showing your middle initial or name only if you intend to use it every time you sign as a Notary Public. List the physical location of your residence, not the address of your employment. Sign the application with an original signature exactly as your name is printed.

Be aware that any misstatement or omission of requested information is cause for the Secretary of State to deny or revoke your commission, as well as to initiate criminal prosecution for lying on the application form.

4. Purchase your bond.

To protect the public from your intentional or unintentional misconduct as a Notary, you must purchase a $5,000 bond in duplicate form from a surety company authorized to do business in the state. You will receive two original bond forms so that you may keep one for your records and file the other with the Secretary of State.

The bond may not be issued more than 60 days before or 30 days after the commission is granted. Both effective and expiration dates must appear on the bond. The expiration date of the bond is always one day less than the effective date four years later. The bond must show your name printed and signed exactly as on your Notary application in two places. The bond must also be countersigned by the authorized bonding company agent in two places on the bond form and properly notarized.

Your oath of office will be on the bond. Make sure there are no blank lines in the bond, or your application will be rejected. You must take the oath and sign the bond before another commissioned Notary who must notarize your signature.

5. Submit your application, bond and fees.

Mail the original application with an original signature, an original notarized bond with original signatures, and a check or money order in the amount of $43.00 (includes the $25 application fee and the $18 Notary bond filing fee) made payable to the Secretary of State at the following address:

    Arizona Secretary of State
    Attention: Notary Section
    1700 W. Washington Street, 7th Floor
    Phoenix, AZ 85007-2888

If you need your commission within a few days, enclose an additional $25 and write "EXPEDITE" clearly on your application and its envelope.

6. Obtain an official Notary seal and journal.

Before you perform any notarial act with your new Notary commission, you must receive your commission certificate from the Secretary of State. You will need a copy of your commission certificate to order an inking rubber stamp Notary seal from a stationery store, office supply store or Notary organization. (See the following section, "Tools of the Trade," for the specific requirements of Arizona law regarding a Notary Public's seal and journal.) ■

Tools of the Trade

Notaries need several tools in order to carry out their duties lawfully and efficiently. These tools are as important to the Notary as a hammer and saw are to the carpenter.

Inking Seal

An Arizona Notary must authenticate all official acts with a seal of office. Its impression must be made in dark ink and must reproduce photographically. It must include the Notary's name (exactly as on the bond and application form), the words "Notary Public," the name of the county where the Notary is commissioned, the expiration date of the Notary's commission, and the Great Seal of the State of Arizona. The state does not provide inking rubber stamp seals, but they are available from stationery or office supply stores or professional Notary organizations like the NNA.

Seal Embosser

The seal embosser makes an indentation on the document that is not photographically reproducible. While the seal embosser is not required by Arizona law, and cannot serve alone as the Notary's official seal, many Arizona Notaries opt to affix an embossment in addition to the legally required inking rubber stamp seal impression. An embossment is often vital on documents sent abroad. In addition, because photocopies of documents can easily pass as originals today, embossment can be used to distinguish an original from a photocopy. Embossing all pages in a document together can also safeguard against later fraudulent substitution or addition of pages.

Journal of Notarial Acts

A Notary is required by law to keep a paper journal of all official acts and record his or her official acts in chronological order. This journal should be a bound book designed specifically for the purpose of recording the details of each notarial act performed, including the signatures of individuals and other information proving the identity of signers and the circumstances of notarizations.

Jurat Stamp

An inking rubber stamp for jurats impresses on an affidavit the wording, "Signed and sworn to (or affirmed) before me on _____ (date) by _____ (name of person making statement)." This wording is stamped below the document's text. Although such a stamp is not required by law, it is more convenient for the Notary than typing or printing the required wording on each document on which the Notary executes a jurat. A stamp is also safer, since critical wording will not be accidentally omitted.

Venue Stamp

An inking rubber venue stamp impresses on a document the location of the notarization in the form "State of _____, County of _____." A venue stamp may be used for acknowledgments, jurats, copy certifications or any other notarial act when otherwise acceptable notarial certificate wording does not include a venue statement.

Fingerprinting Device

Although Arizona Law does not require a signer to affix a thumbprint in the Notary's journal, Notaries increasingly are asking signers to do so. A thumbprint serves as proof that a particular individual did or did not appear, thereby deterring fraud. Many Notaries opt for the convenience of an inexpensive inkless device that allows a thumb- or fingerprint to be printed quickly and efficiently.

Notarial Certificates

The notarial certificate contains the required wording that, when completed by a commissioned Notary, recites the facts attested by a Notary in a particular notarization. Occasionally a document will have no notarial wording or the provided wording will not match the state's requirements or there will be no room for the Notary's seal. For your convenience, the NNA provides preprinted notarial certificates for acknowledgments, jurats and copy certifications.

Errors and Omissions Insurance

Notary errors and omissions (E&O) insurance provides protection for Notaries who are sued for damages resulting from unintentional mistakes. In the event of a lawsuit, the E&O insurance company will provide and pay for the Notary's legal counsel and absorb any damages levied by a court or agreed to in a settlement, up to the policy coverage limit. The Notary is not required to repay any money that the insurance company pays out on a claim. Keep in mind, though, that errors and omissions insurance does not cover the Notary for intentional misconduct. ■

As a full-service organization, the National Notary Association makes available to Arizona Notaries all notarial items required by law, custom and convenience.

10 Most-Asked Questions

Every Notary has a question or two about whether and how to notarize. But certain questions pop up again and again. These top 10 are asked repeatedly at the National Notary Association's seminars, its annual National Conference of Notaries Public and through its Notary Information Service Hotline.

As with most questions about notarization, the answers to these 10 are not always a simple yes or no. Sometimes the answer is "It depends."

Here's what every Notary wants to know:

1. May I notarize a will?

It depends. Often, it is not the will itself that is notarized, but the signatures of witnesses on accompanying affidavits. Under specific circumstances, an individual may "self-prove" a will before witnesses and a Notary Public.

But you should notarize a signature on a will only if clear instructions from an attorney and a notarial certificate are provided. If you notarize a will drafted by a would-be testator who has not received legal advice, he or she may believe that notarization will make the will legal and valid. However, even when notarized, such homemade wills may be worthless because the testators failed to obtain the proper number of witnesses or omitted important information. In fact, notarization may actually void an otherwise properly executed handwritten (holographic) will, because courts have occasionally held that any writing on the document other than the testator's invalidates the will.

2. May I notarize for a stranger with no identification?

Yes. If you cannot identify a signer based upon personal

knowledge or identification documents (ID cards), you may rely on the oath or affirmation of a credible person who personally knows the document signer. A credible person should be someone the Notary believes to be trustworthy and impartial. If a person has a financial interest in the document being notarized, that individual cannot be a reliably impartial witness.

Two types of credible persons or credible identifying witnesses may be used. The first is a person whom you know. In this case, the satisfactory evidence of the credible person's identity is your personal knowledge, resulting in the establishment of a chain of personal knowledge from you through the credible identifying witness to the signer. The second type of credible person is one whom you do not know. This credible person must present you with a valid ID card that will serve as satisfactory evidence of identity.

When no credible person is available to identify a stranger without an acceptable identification card, you may have no choice but to refer the signer to a personally known Notary or to a friend who personally knows a Notary.

3. May I notarize a photograph?

No. To simply affix a signature and seal on a photograph is improper, because a Notary's signature and seal must appear only on a notarial certificate accompanying a statement signed by another person. However, you may notarize an individual's signature on a written statement referring to an accompanying or attached photograph. If the photograph is large enough, the statement and notarial certificate might appear on its reverse side. Such formats might be acceptable when "notarized" photos are requested by people seeking medical or health licenses, or by legal residents renewing foreign passports.

A word of caution here: You should always hesitate to notarize a photo-bearing card or document that could be used as a bogus "official" ID.

4. Is there a recommended practice I should follow if there's no room for my seal or if it smears?

Yes. If there is not enough room on a document for your seal and signature, then you should complete and attach a "loose certificate," a separate sheet of paper containing the notarial wording, your seal and your signature. You should neatly print or type on the document that a loose certificate is attached.

ARIZONA NOTARY LAW PRIMER

In addition, you must print or type on the loose certificate a description of the document that includes at least the title or type of the document, the document date, the number of pages, and the name of any additional document signers not named in the notarial certificate.

Missing, illegible and overprinted Notary seal impressions are the most frequent reasons a document is rejected by a receiving agency. But you should never attempt to fix an imperfect seal impression with a pen or correction fluid or both. This may be viewed as evidence of tampering and cause the document to be rejected by a receiving agency. Instead, if an initial seal impression is unreadable and there is room on the document, you may affix another impression nearby. The illegibility of the first seal impression will indicate why a second impression was necessary. You should record in your journal that you applied a second impression.

5. May I notarize signatures on faxes or photocopies of documents?

It depends. If a photocopy or fax was signed with pen and ink, you may notarize the signature. But a signature that was photocopied or faxed may never be notarized, because it is impossible to determine the validity of such a signature. It is far too easy to create fraudulent documents on a computer or by cutting a signature off of one document, pasting it onto another and then photocopying or faxing the altered document.

Notaries should be aware that sometimes public recorders will not accept notarized photocopies or faxes, even if the signatures are original, because the text of the documents may be too faint to adequately reproduce in microfilming.

6. May I notarize for customers only?

No. As a public official, you are commissioned to notarize for anyone who reasonably requests service, not just the customers or clients of your business. Even when your employer paid for your commission fees and notarial supplies, your duty is to serve all members of the public without discriminating. Arizona does not commission "Notaries Private."

It is ethically improper — although not explicitly prohibited by statute — to discriminate between customers and noncustomers in offering or refusing to offer notarial services and in charging or not charging fees. Since a Notary may not refuse a reasonable and a lawful request for a notarization, and must treat all people fairly and equally, you should provide services to both customers and noncustomers. Discrimination against anyone who presents a lawful request for notarization simply is not a suitable policy for a public official appointed to serve all of the public equally.

7. May I notarize a document in a language I can't read?

It depends. As long as the notarial certificate is worded and completed in a language that you read, write and understand, you may notarize signatures on documents written in languages you cannot read. If the certificate is in a language that you cannot read, write and understand, however, you must add and complete the appropriate notarial wording in a language that you do read, write and understand.

While notarizing a document you cannot read is permitted, there are difficulties and dangers in doing this. You may have difficulty in making an accurate journal entry if you cannot read the title of the document. Beyond that, you have no way of determining whether the document is legitimate or fraudulent. As a result, you might not be able to prevent a fraud from occurring and might even unknowingly perform an illegal act.

8. May I certify a copy of a birth certificate?

No. While Arizona Notaries are authorized to certify copies, they are specifically prohibited from certifying copies of vital records, public records or publicly recorded documents that are available as certified copies from an official source other than a Notary Public. Only an officer in a bureau of vital statistics may certify a copy of a vital public record, such as a birth certificate. Your "certification" of a copy of this type of record could lend credibility to what is actually a counterfeit or altered document. In Arizona, Notaries may only properly certify copies of original personal papers such as college diplomas, letters and in-house business documents.

9. Must a document be signed in my presence?

It depends. Documents requiring acknowledgments normally do not need to be signed in your presence. When performing an acknowledgment, you certify only that the signer of the document personally appeared before you at the time of the notarization, was identified by you and acknowledged (declared or stated) to you that he or she freely signed for the purposes stated in the document.

On the other hand, documents requiring a jurat must be signed in your presence, as dictated by the typical jurat wording, "Subscribed and sworn (or affirmed) before me ..." When executing a jurat, you certify that the person making the jurat personally appeared before you, was identified by you, signed the document in your presence and was given an oath or affirmation by you.

10. May I notarize for a family member?

It depends. Arizona law states that a Notary may not notarize for anyone related by marriage or adoption. While this means that you could notarize for someone related by blood, such as a sibling, the Secretary of State recommends that you never notarize the signature of any close family member in order to avoid any appearance of partiality or beneficial interest. ∎

Steps to Proper Notarization

When Notaries perform a notarial act, they are expected to exercise what is known as "reasonable care." Reasonable care is the level of attentiveness and precaution expected of a person of ordinary intelligence. The first rule of reasonable care is strict adherence to all laws governing Notaries and notarization. Second, Arizona Notaries should put into practice all of the Secretary of State's recommendations in the state-issued *Arizona Notary Public Reference Manual*. In situations not explicitly covered by statute or recommendation, a Notary should make every effort to use common sense and behave in a responsible and ethical fashion, following the accepted best practices for that situation.

As a Notary, you should exercise reasonable care not only because failure to do so may result in disciplinary measures or a lawsuit to recover financial damages caused by an error, but also because your actions may facilitate a fraud that harms the very members of the public whom you have been commissioned to protect. If, on the other hand, you can convincingly show that you used reasonable care when performing a notarization, the public will be protected and you will be shielded from liability in the event that the notarization is challenged.

The following 14-step checklist will help you to apply the principles of reasonable care.

1. Require every signer to personally appear.

The signer must appear in person before the Notary on the date and in the county stated in the notarial certificate. "Personal appearance" means that the signer is in the Notary's physical presence — face to face in the same room. Communication between the Notary and the signer cannot be established over the phone, from another room, through the mail or through a third person.

2. Visually scan the document.

Notaries are not required to read the documents they notarize, and they are not responsible for the accuracy of the contents. However, you should note certain important particulars about each document for recording in the journal of notarial acts, such as its title and date. You should count and record in your journal the number of pages in the document. This can show whether pages are later fraudulently added or removed.

3. Look for blank spaces.

As an Arizona Notary, you must not notarize a jurat with blank spaces in it. You should visually scan every document for blank spaces, since incomplete documents have a great potential for fraudulent misuse. A borrower, for example, might sign a promissory note with blank spaces, trusting the lender to fill in the amount borrowed, only to discover later that the lender has written in an amount in excess of what was actually borrowed.

The document signer should fill in any spaces left in a document. If the signer does not know how the blanks should be filled in, then you should ask him or her to contact the document issuing agency. If the blanks are inapplicable and intended to be left unfilled, you should ask the signer to line through each space using ink or write "Not Applicable" or "N/A."

4. Check the document's date.

For acknowledgments, the date of signing on a document must either precede or be the same as the date of notarization; it may not follow it. A document whose signature date follows the date on its notarial certificate risks rejection by a recorder or other intended recipient, who may question how the signature could have been notarized before it was placed on the document. For a jurat, the document signing date and notarization date must be the same.

5. Make a careful identification.

Because the essence of the notarial act is verification of a signer's identity, you should identify every document signer either through personal knowledge, reliable ID cards or the word of a credible person under oath. Although the National Notary Association recommends that a signer be positively identified each and every time he or she appears, an Arizona Notary may not require a signer to present identification — or sign the Notary's journal — if that person has already proven identity and signed the journal within the previous six months.

When using ID cards, you should examine them closely to detect alteration, counterfeiting or evidence that they have been issued to an impostor. You should not rely on a type of card with which you are unfamiliar, unless you check it against a reference such as the *U.S. Identification Manual* or the *ID Checking Guide*.

6. Verify that the signer understands the document and is signing it voluntarily.

A careful Notary will be certain not only of the signer's identity, but also of the signer's willingness to sign the document and his or her ability to understand it. While Arizona Notaries are not expressly required by law to determine awareness, it is in the public interest for you to make a commonsense judgment about these issues, because notarizing for someone who does not understand the consequences of the transaction or has been coerced into signing may allow a fraud to occur.

Determining that a principal is signing the document voluntarily without duress or undue influence is relatively easy. You simply ask the signer if he or she has signed or is about to sign the document willingly and then carefully watch for any indications to the contrary. If you suspect that a signer is being forced or coerced into signing against his or her will, then you should refuse to perform the notarization.

Ascertaining the signer's awareness of what he or she is signing can be established by asking the signer simple questions about the document. If the signer can respond intelligibly to these questions, then you may proceed with the notarization. If you are unsure of a signer's understanding, then you may refuse service.

7. Check all signatures.

The various signatures you will witness or examine during a notarization present opportunities for you to detect a forgery. If the signer presents an identification card, you should compare the signature on the ID with the signature on the document to make sure that they are reasonably similar. The signature in the Notary's journal should also match the signatures on the document and on the ID. If the signer appears to labor over the signature in the journal, that may indicate a forgery in progress.

8. Keep a journal of notarial acts.

Keeping a journal is mandatory for all Notaries in Arizona. If a notarized document is lost or altered, or if certain facts about the transaction are later challenged, your journal becomes valuable evidence. It can protect the rights of all parties to a transaction and help you defend yourself against false accusations.

An identified signer who appears before the same Notary for second and subsequent notarizations within one six-month period is not required to sign the Notary's journal after the first time, but the National Notary Association strongly recommends that you ask the signer to sign each time.

You must include in each journal entry the date and type of each notarial act; the date and type of document; the signature, printed name and address of the signer; a description of the satisfactory evidence identifying each person; and the fee you charged, if any. You may also enter any other pertinent data, such as the time of day of the notarization, any representative capacity the signer is claiming or the reason(s) for refusing to notarize or not completing a given notarial act. Although Arizona Notaries are not required to ask signers to leave a thumbprint in the journal, you may do so as a means to deter to fraud.

9. Complete the journal entry first.

In order to make a complete and accurate record of the notarial act, you should enter the information in the journal at the actual time of the notarial act, not before and not after. As soon as the signer appears before you, you can begin your journal entry by recording the general information about the transaction. You should complete the journal entry entirely before filling out the notarial certificate. This prevents a signer from leaving before the important public record of the notarization is made in the journal.

10. Make sure the document has notarial wording.

An Arizona Notary may not notarize a document that does not have notarial wording. If a notarial certificate does not come with the document, you should ask the document signer what type of notarization is required. You may then print or type the appropriate notarial wording on the document or attach a preprinted loose certificate. If the signer does not know what type of notarization is required, he or she should contact the document's issuing or receiving agency to determine this. Do not make this decision unless you are also an attorney.

11. Be attentive to details.

When completing the notarial certificate, you need to make sure that the venue statement is present and that it correctly identifies the place of notarization. If the venue statement is missing, then you must add it, either by hand or with a venue stamp. If the venue is preprinted and incorrect, you should either line through the incorrect state and/or county and then neatly print the proper information, or cross out the entire venue statement and then replace it using an inking rubber venue stamp. In either case, you should initial and date the change.

You should also pay attention to any text on the notarial certificate that indicates the number and gender of the document signers, as well as how they were identified. You should line through or cross out any inapplicable text — for example, plurals and pronouns that do not apply to the signer(s) in question.

12. Affix your signature and seal properly.

You must sign exactly the same name as that appearing on your commissioned name on file with the Secretary of State's office. If your title, "Notary Public," is not preprinted below or next to your signature, you should print it on the certificate. And you must not forget to affix your official seal — a common reason for rejection of a document by a recorder.

You should place the seal impression as close to your signature as possible without overprinting it. The Arizona Secretary of State recommends that the official inking seal be placed just below the notarial wording and to the left, if possible. To prevent illegibility, you should not place your seal or signature over printed material or a document signer's signature. However, if there is no room on the document for your seal, the Secretary of State's office recommends affixing it over the preprinted wording.

13. Protect loose certificates.

If you have to attach a notarial certificate, you should securely staple it to the document's signature page. You can protect against the fraudulent removal of attached certificates by embossing them together with the document.

Effective July 20, 2011, you must also include a description of the document on any notarial certificate that you attach as a separate sheet of paper to the document. The description must include at least the title or type of the document, the document date, the number of pages, and the names of any additional document signers not named in the notarial certificate.

14. Don't give advice.

Every state prohibits those who are not attorneys from practicing law. You should never choose the type of certificate or notarization that a document needs, prepare or complete documents for others, or give advice on any matter relating to a document unless you are an attorney or a professional certified or licensed in a relevant area of expertise. These decisions can have important legal ramifications, and you could be held liable for any damages resulting from an incorrectly chosen certificate, notarization or document wording. ■

Notary Laws Explained

In layperson's language, this chapter discusses and clarifies key parts of the laws of Arizona that regulate Notaries Public. Most of these laws are reprinted in full in "Arizona Laws Pertaining to Notaries Public" beginning on page 86. In the text that follows, these abbreviations are used:

<u>ARS</u>: *Arizona Revised Statutes,* the enacted laws regulating the activities of Notaries Public

<u>AAC</u>: *Arizona Administrative Code,* the rules pertaining to Notaries Public and carrying the full force and effect of law

<u>ANPRM</u>: *Arizona Notary Public Reference Manual* (July 2010), a guide for Notaries by the Arizona Secretary of State's office

The term "Notary" used throughout this chapter also includes the term "electronic Notary." In Arizona, there are separate Notary and electronic Notary commissions. Mostly identical rules and procedures for each are contained in separate articles of the *Arizona Revised Statutes.* Statute citations for both are noted throughout this *Primer.*

THE NOTARY COMMISSION

Authority of Secretary of State

<u>Notary Appointments</u>. Arizona's Secretary of State appoints, regulates and maintains records on the state's Notaries (*ARS* 41-126 and 41-312).

Notary Database. The Secretary maintains a database of Notaries on the official website, www.azsos.gov. The database is searchable by commission number, first and last name, business name, business address and commission expiration date range.

Notary Records and Journals. The Secretary of State is required by law to keep all records and journals of Arizona Notaries who are no longer serving as Notaries on deposit in the Secretary's office for five years after the date of the last notarial act in the records. The Secretary of State may provide certified copies of these records upon request, charging the same fees that are allowed by law to Notaries for copy certifications (ARS 41-317[B] and 41-359[B]).

Application for Commission

Qualifications. To become a Notary in Arizona, the applicant must (ARS 41-312[E] and 41-353[F]):

1) Be 18 years of age or older

2) Be a citizen or legal permanent resident of the United States

3) Be a legal Arizona resident for income tax purposes, claiming a residence in the state as his or her primary residence on state and federal tax returns

4) Not have been convicted of a felony, unless his or her civil rights have been restored

5) Be able to read and write English

Possession of Civil Rights. Being in possession of one's civil rights means that one's activities are not legally restricted as a result of a felony conviction or other legal proceeding. A person with a previous felony conviction may apply to become a Notary if his or her civil rights have been legally restored. Applicants who have been convicted of a felony must submit with the Notary application the court papers showing that their civil rights have been restored. However, the Arizona Secretary of State may deny a Notary commission to any person judged unfit to perform notarial duties. If the conviction has a reasonable relationship to the functions of the office of Notary Public, the Secretary of State likely will deny a commission (ANPRM).

Application Misstatement. An applicant's substantial and material misstatement or omission in the application for a Notary commission is reason for the Secretary of State to deny, suspend or revoke a commission (*ARS* 41-330[A][1] and 41-368[A][1]).

Application Fee. For both first-time and renewal applicants, the fee for processing the application for an Arizona Notary commission is $25 (*ARS* 41-126[A][2]), plus an additional $18 for filing the bond and oath of office (*ARS* 41-126[A][11]). Checks for $43 should be made payable to "Secretary of State." An expedited application costs an additional $25 (*ARS* 41-126[B]).

Upon approval of the application the Secretary of State will notify the applicant of his or her appointment. The applicant then has 20 days to take the oath prescribed by law and file a bond if he or she has not already done so. Once the applicant files the official oath and bond, the Secretary of State will send the Notary his or her commission papers (*ARS* 41-312[B]).

For application provisions related to electronic Notary commissions, see "Electronic Notary Commission," pages 67–68.

Reference Manual Requirement. Each Notary commissioned in the state is required to keep a reference manual that describes the duties, authority and ethical responsibilities of Notaries (*ARS* 41-312[E][5] and 41-353[F][5]). The current version of the *Arizona Notary Public Reference Manual* may be downloaded and printed from the Secretary of State's website (www.azsos.gov), or requested by phone (602-542-4758), eMail (notary@azsos.gov) or regular mail.

Notary Training Course. Tthe Arizona Secretary of State may require applicants for a Notary commission to attend a training course before receiving their commissions. The Secretary may also require renewing Notaries to attend a training course within the ninety days preceding renewal of their commissions. The Secretary may assess a fee for such training (*ARS* 41-312[H] and 41-353[I]).

Notary Bond
Requirement. Each Arizona Notary is required to obtain a four-year, $5,000 bond, in duplicate. Electronic Notaries' bonds are $25,000. The Notary applicant must have the forms notarized and then should submit one to the Secretary of State with his or her

application. He or she should keep the second form in his or her records (*ARS* 315[A], *AAC* R2-12-1103 and *ANPRM*).

Bonds must be purchased from a state-licensed surety. Sureties licensed in Arizona may be Notary bonding companies, insurance companies or Notary organizations. The surety agrees to pay damages to anyone who suffers financially because of the Notary's improper acts, intentional or not, in the event the Notary does not have the financial resources to pay these damages. A deposit of funds may not be made in lieu of a surety bond (*ARS* 41-312[B], 41-315[A] and *AAC* R2-12-1103).

Protects Public. The bond does not protect the Notary, but rather protects the public from a Notary's misconduct or negligence. A Notary and the surety company bonding the Notary may be sued by any person who has been harmed by the Notary's official acts. The surety is liable only up to the $5,000 amount of the bond ($25,000 for electronic Notaries) and will seek compensation from the Notary for any damages it has to pay out on the Notary's behalf. A Notary, however, may be found liable for any amount of money.

Form of the Bond. The Notary bond must not be issued more than 60 days before or 30 days after the Notary's commissioning date (*ARS* 41-315[B]). The bond must display effective and expiration dates, with the expiration date always four years minus one day after the effective date of the bond (*ANPRM*).

The bond must display the applicant's printed name and must be signed in two places exactly as the applicant signs the application form. The bond must be countersigned by the bonding company's authorized agent in two places on the bond form. Since the bond contains the Notary's oath of office (see "Oath of Office," below), it must be properly notarized with jurat language (*ARS* 41-312[B]). It must contain no blank lines.

Filing the Bond. The Secretary of State recommends that the notarized original bond be filed with the Notary application (*ANPRM*). Statute requires a Notary to file the bond with the Secretary of State within 20 days after the Secretary of State notifies a person of his or her appointment as a Notary (*ARS* 38-233[B], *ARS* 41-312[B] and 41-315[A]). The Notary commission does not take effect until this filing has been done (*ARS* 41-315[A]).

NOTARY LAWS EXPLAINED

Oath of Office

Requirement. Each person applying for a Notary commission must take an oath of office in the presence of a Notary Public or other oath-administering official. The oath of office appears on the Notary bond (*ARS* 38-233[B]). The Secretary of State recommends that the applicant file the original bond and oath with the application (*ANPRM*). Statute requires a Notary to file the oath with the Secretary of State within 20 days after receiving notification of appointment as a Notary. (*ARS* 41-312[B], 41-353[B]). The Notary commission does not take effect until this filing has been done *ARS* 41-315[A]).

Official Record. The Notary's oath of office is maintained as an official record for a period of five years after the Notary's commission expires or has been terminated (*ARS* 38-233[F]).

Notary Commission Certificate

Issuance. A commission certificate is an official document issued by the Secretary of State's Office that certifies the appointment of a Notary Public. The commission certificate is the Notary's proof that he or she is commissioned as a Notary Public in the state of Arizona (*ARS* 41-311[2]). Notary commission certificates for new and renewing Notaries are issued by the Secretary of State's office to the applicant once the Secretary receives the bond and oath (*ARS* 41-312[B] and *ANPRM*).

Commission Certificate Copy. A Notary must present a photocopy of his or her commission certificate to a vendor in order to obtain an official seal. The seal vendor must keep this commission photocopy on file for four years (*ARS* 41-321[A]).

While a Notary may display his or her original commission certificate, he or she should not provide a copy of the commission certificate to anyone. A person requiring proof of a Notary's authority may contact the Secretary of State's office (*ANPRM*).

Jurisdiction

Notaries. Arizona Notaries may perform official acts throughout the state of Arizona but not beyond the state borders. A Notary may not witness a signing outside Arizona and then return to the state to perform the notarization. An Arizona Notary must perform all parts of a notarial act at the same time and place within the state of Arizona (*ARS* 41-312[A] and *ANPRM*).

25

Electronic Notaries. Arizona electonic Notaries may perform electronic acts anywhere within the United States (*ARS* 41-352[F]).

Term of Office

Four-Year Term. Beginning with the date specified on the commission certificate, a Notary's term of office is four years. The commission ends at midnight on the expiration date (*ARS* 41-312[A], 41-353[A] and *ANPRM*).

Change of Address

Notification. Whenever a Notary changes his or her mailing, business or residence address, the Notary must inform the Secretary of State of the address change within 30 days by certified mail or other means that would provide a receipt of delivery (*ARS* 41-323[A] and 41-364). The Notary must also include in the signed notice both the new and old addresses. Use the "Notary Public Address/Name Change Form" found on the Secretary of State's website at www.azsos.gov/business_services/ or in the back of the *Reference Manual*. Any person who fails to notify the Secretary of State of a change in mailing or residence address may be subject to a $25 civil penalty, which must be paid before the Notary can be commissioned to a new term (*ARS* 41-323 and 41-364[C]).

Failure to Maintain Residency. Moving out of the state and failing to maintain Arizona residency has the same effect as resignation of one's Notary commission. The Notary who moves out of Arizona must follow the procedures described under "Resignation" on page 27 (*ARS* 38-294[2] and *ANPRM*).

Change of Name

Two Options: A Notary Public who changes his or her surname may either apply for a new commission under his or her new name and purchase a new seal, or continue to use his or her prior name. If a Notary wants to use the prior name, he or she should sign the new name on the line designated for the Notary Public's signature on the notarial certificate, and then, immediately below that signature, sign the name under which he or she was commissioned. A Notary choosing to sign his or her previous name must use the seal and commission in that name and may wait until that commission expires to change his or her name (*ARS* 41-327, 41-365 and *ANPRM*).

Notification. No matter which option is chosen, a Notary who changes his or her surname must notify the Secretary of State's office within 30 days of the change of surname by filing the "Notary Public Address/Name Change Form," found in the Reference Manual or on the Secretary of State's website. Failure to notify the Secretary of State of this change of surname is evidence of the Notary's failure to fully and faithfully discharge the duties of a Notary (*ARS* 41-327 and 41-365).

Reappointment

Procedure. There is no automatic renewal process for a commission. A Notary wishing to renew his or her commission should submit a renewal application, new bond and filing fees to the Secretary of State's office 60 days prior to the expiration of his or her commission. The Arizona Secretary of State may require renewing Notaries to attend a training course within the 90 days preceding renewal of their commissions. The Secretary may assess a fee for such training (*ARS* 41-312[H] and 41-363[I]).

A Notary may continue to notarize until midnight of the expiration date of a current commission (*ANPRM*).

Resignation

Procedure. If a Notary has let his or her commission expire and has not received a renewal commission from the Secretary of State's office, he or she may not notarize documents (*ANPRM*).

A Notary commissioned by the Arizona Secretary of State's office may resign a commission at any time. A Notary who chooses to resign must notify the Governor in writing (*ARS* 38-294[2]). A form letter is available online at the Secretary of State's website at www.azsos.gov/business_services/. Copies of the resignation letter should be sent by certified mail to the Secretary of State, and as a courtesy, to the Notary's bond company (*ANPRM*).

Delivery of Seal and Records. A Notary Public who has allowed a commission to expire or who resigns a commission must deliver his or her Notary Public seal, journal, and other Notary records to the Secretary of State's office with a cover letter within three months of the commission's expiration or his or her resignation. The Notary should use certified mail or other means providing a receipt. (See "Disposal of Notary Records," pages 49–50.) If the items are not delivered in this time period, the

Notary shall be fined between $50 and $500 by the Secretary of State's office (*ARS* 41-317[A] and 41-359[A]).

Termination of Employment. If a Notary Public's employment is terminated or he or she leaves that employment, the Notary Public may do any of the following:

- Continue to notarize as a public servant

- Resign his or her commission

- Let the commission expire

If the Notary Public chooses to resign or let the commission expire he or she must follow the above procedures to surrender his or her Notary seal and journal to the Secretary of State's office (*ANPRM*).

Death of Notary

Representative Must Notify State. In the event that a Notary dies during his or her term of commission, the Notary's personal representative or executor should notify the Secretary of State's office. Every Notary should instruct or leave instructions for his or her personal representative to perform the preceding duties as required by law (*ARS* 41-317[A], 41-359[A] and *ANPRM*).

Delivery of Seal and Records. Within three months after being designated, the deceased Notary's personal representative must deliver the Notary's seal, journal and any other notarial records to the Secretary of State's office by certified mail or other means which would provide a receipt. The Notary's representative should include a cover letter with the items. Failure to deliver the records to the Secretary of State's office within three months may result in a fine ranging from $50 to $500 (*ARS* 41-317[A] and 41-359[A]).

OFFICIAL NOTARIAL ACTS

Authorized Acts

Notaries may perform the following notarial acts (*ANPRM, ARS* 41-313[A], 41-320 and 41-355):

- Acknowledgments, certifying that a signer personally appeared before the Notary, was identified by the Notary,

NOTARY LAWS EXPLAINED

and acknowledged having signed the document (See pages 30–34).

- Copy Certifications, attesting that a photocopy is a true, complete and correct copy of an original (See pages 35–36).

- Oaths and Affirmations, witnessing solemn promises to a Supreme Being (oaths) or solemn promises on one's own personal honor (affirmations) (See pages 36–38).

- Jurats, as found in affidavits and other sworn documents, certifying that the signer personally appeared before the Notary, was positively identified by the Notary, signed in the Notary's presence and took an oath or affirmation from the Notary (See pages 38–40).

- Protests, certifying that a written promise to pay, such as a bill of exchange, was not honored (See page 40–41).

Unauthorized Acts

Notarize Own Signature. Notaries are not permitted to notarize their own signatures (*ARS* 41-328, 41-366[B] and *ANPRM*).

Notarize Signatures of Certain Relatives. A Notary may not notarize for anyone related by marriage or adoption (*ARS* 41-328[B] and *ARS* 41-366[B]).

Act as Witness and Notary. A Notary may not act as both witness and Notary on the same document, except when notarizing a signature by mark (*ANPRM*).

Certify Copies of Recordable Documents. A Notary is not authorized to certify a copy of a document that is a public record or publicly recordable, including birth and death certificates, marriage licenses, divorce papers, court records and real estate deeds (*ARS* 41-311[3] and *ANPRM*).

Execute a Jurat on an Incomplete Document. A Notary may not execute a jurat on a document that has not been signed where a signature line is provided, or that has no notarial certificate or that has other obvious blanks or missing pages (*ARS* 41-311[5], 41-328[A] and 41-366[A]).

Execute Depositions. Arizona Notaries do not have the authority to take a deposition — that is, to write down the words of a witness (deponent) in a lawsuit or other official proceeding. However, a Notary still has the power to administer the oath or affirmation to a deponent who is about to give oral testimony that will be written down by someone else, or to execute the jurat at the end of an already prepared deposition. In fact, when shorthand or court reporters cross state lines to take depositions, they often must call on a local Notary to administer the required oath to the deponent.

Execute Proofs of Execution by Subscribing Witness. An Arizona Notary does not have the authority to perform a proof of execution by subscribing witness, an authorized act in some states in which a person (the subscribing witness) personally appears and swears to the Notary that another person (the principal) signed a document. Proofs of execution are listed in the state's Property Code (*ARS* 33-501) as an act Notaries may perform, but since the *Arizona Notary Public Reference Manual* emphatically states that a signer must be in the Notary's presence at the time of notarization, a proof may not be completed.

Perform Marriage Ceremonies. Arizona Notaries have no authority to perform marriage ceremonies unless they are also clergy members or officials given the power by state law.

Acknowledgments

A Common Notarial Act. Acknowledgments are the most common forms of notarization. Typically, they are executed on documents such as deeds and other documents affecting real property that will be publicly recorded by a county recorder.

Purpose. In executing an acknowledgment, the Notary certifies three things (*ARS* 33-503, 41-311[1], 41-313[B][1] and 41-355[B][1]):

1) The signer personally appeared before the Notary on the date and in the county indicated on the notarial certificate;

2) The signer was positively identified by the Notary through either personal knowledge or satisfactory evidence (see "Identifying Document Signers," page 41); and

3) The signer acknowledged having signed the document for the purposes stated in the document.

Terminology. "Acknowledged before me" means that the signer appeared before the Notary and acknowledged signing the document for the stated purposes, and that the Notary identified the signer as the person named in the document. It also means that, when applicable, the signer acknowledged that he or she had the authority to sign as corporate officer, partner, attorney in fact or in another representative capacity for the entity or person named (*ARS* 33-505).

In discussing the notarial act of acknowledgment, it is important to use the proper terminology. The signer acknowledges his or her signature; the Notary takes the signer's acknowledgment.

Notary Need Not Witness Signing. The signer is not required to sign the document in the Notary's presence for an acknowledgment. The signer may choose to pre-sign the document or sign it in the Notary's presence. Even if a document has been pre-signed, however, the document signer must be in the Notary's presence at the time the Notary performs the notarization to acknowledge the signature. Because the Notary is attesting to the genuineness of the signature, the Notary may not perform an acknowledgment that will be signed at a later time (*ANPRM*).

Capacity of Signer. Besides acknowledging his or her signature, a person signing in a representative capacity, such as corporate officer, trustee, partner to a partnership, attorney in fact or other capacity must additionally acknowledge to the Notary that he or she does, in fact, have the authority to sign the document in the stated capacity (*ARS* 33-505). The Notary may ask for proof of authority to sign. A person signing as a partner, for example, may be asked to present a copy of the partnership agreement.

Foreign-Language Signatures. Effective July 20, 2011, the signer whose signature is being acknowledged before a Notary must sign the document in a language the Notary understands. For example, a signer who wishes to sign in Chinese may do so only if the Notary also understands Chinese (*ARS* 41-313[B][2]).

Married Women. A woman's marital status has no effect on her acknowledgment before a Notary. A Notary takes the acknowledgment made by a married woman just as if she were unmarried (*ARS* 33-512).

Who May Take. In addition to Notaries, the following officials may also take acknowledgments and proofs within their Arizona jurisdictions: a judge of a court of record, a clerk or deputy clerk of a court having a seal, a recorder of deeds, a justice of the peace and a county recorder (*ARS* 33-511).

Statutory "Short-Form" Certificates. Arizona law provides five statutory short-form acknowledgment certificates that accommodate signers acting in an individual capacity or in one of several representative capacities.

- Statutory Individual Short-Form Acknowledgment Certificate for an individual signing on his or her own behalf (*ARS* 33-506[1]):

State of Arizona)
)
County of _____)

The foregoing instrument was acknowledged before me this _____ [date] by _____ [name of signer].

[Seal] _____ [Signature of Notary]
        Notary Public

- Statutory Corporate Short-Form Acknowledgment Certificate for a corporate officer or agent acting on behalf of a corporation (*ARS* 33-506[2]):

State of Arizona)
)
County of _____)

The foregoing instrument was acknowledged before me this ___ [date] by _____ [name of officer or agent], _____ (title of officer or agent) of _____ [name of corporation], a[n] _____ [state of incorporation] corporation, on behalf of the corporation.

[Seal] _____ [Signature of Notary]
        Notary Public

- Statutory Partnership Short-Form Acknowledgment Certificate for a partner or agent acting on behalf of a partnership (*ARS* 33-506[3]):

State of Arizona)
)
County of _____)

The foregoing instrument was acknowledged before me this _____ [date] by _____ [name of partner or agent], partner/agent on behalf of _____ [name of partnership], a partnership.

[Seal] _____ [Signature of Notary]
      Notary Public

- Statutory Attorney in Fact Short-Form Acknowledgment Certificate for an attorney in fact acting on behalf of a principal (*ARS* 33-506[4]):

State of Arizona)
)
County of _____)

The foregoing instrument was acknowledged before me this _____ [date] by _____ [name of attorney in fact] as attorney in fact on behalf of _____ [name of principal].

[Seal] _____ [Signature of Notary]
      Notary Public

- Statutory Representative Short-Form Acknowledgment Certificate for a public officer, trustee, or personal representative acting on behalf of a public entity, trust or principal (*ARS* 33-506[5]):

State of Arizona)
)
County of _____)

The foregoing instrument was acknowledged before me this _____ [date] by _____ [name of representative], _____ [title of representative].

[Seal] _____ [Signature of Notary]
      Notary Public

ARIZONA NOTARY LAW PRIMER

Similar Certificates Allowed. Arizona law also allows other certificate wordings as long as the certificate is in a form prescribed by Arizona law, is in a form prescribed by the state law where the acknowledgment was taken or contains the words "acknowledged before me" or the equivalent (*ARS* 33-504 and 33-506).

For example, if a signer asks a Notary to perform an acknowledgment but the document does not contain a notarial certificate with language for an acknowledgment, the Notary may use the following sample acknowledgment wording (*ANPRM*):

State of Arizona   )
)
County of _____   )

On this _____ day of _____, 20___, before me personally appeared _____, whose identity was proven to me on the basis of satisfactory evidence to be the person who he or she claims to be, and acknowledged that he or she signed the above/attached document.

(seal)

_____
Notary Public

Out-of-State Acknowledgments. Acknowledgment certificates completed outside of Arizona by Notaries of another state in accordance with the laws of that state may be recorded in Arizona. However, acknowledgments completed in Arizona for use out of the state must substantially comply with the acknowledgment requirements of Arizona (*ARS* 33-504).

Correcting Acknowledgment Certificates. If any part of the notarial certificate is incorrect, the Notary should either cross out and initial the incorrect words with ink or cross out the entire wording and type or write in the correct wording. A Notary should not attempt to erase or use correction fluid or tape (*ANPRM*).

If an error is discovered later, any party may correct a notarial certificate that was incorrectly completed if that party brings action in the Superior Court to obtain a judgment for correction (*ARS* 33-513).

Copy Certifications

Purpose. Arizona Notaries have authority to certify that a copy of an original document is a true, complete and correct reproduction of the document that was copied. The Notary's authority to certify copies is limited to documents that are not public records or publicly recordable (*ARS* 41-311[3] and *ANPRM*). A common request is to certify a copy of a college diploma, since only one such document exists and most people do not want to risk parting with the original when proof of their graduate status is requested by a prospective employer or school.

Notaries also may certify copies of entries in their own official journals of notarial acts (*ARS* 41-319[A]). (See "Inspection or Certified Copies of Journal Entry," page 48.)

Physical Presence Required. A person requesting a copy certification must be physically present before the Notary at the time the copy certification is performed (*ARS* 41-313[B][1]).

Prohibited Documents. Arizona Notaries are prohibited from certifying copies of recordable documents, such as deeds. Look for the words "Filed" or "Received" that are stamped by the recorder on such documents. A document does not have to be recorded, but merely recordable, for the Notary to be prohibited from making a certified copy (*ANPRM*).

Arizona Notaries are expressly prohibited from certifying copies of birth, death or marriage certificates or divorce decrees because these are vital public records. Only officials in a bureau of vital statistics or other public-record office may certify originals or copies of such certificates. (See "Bureaus of Vital Statistics," pages 126–130.) A Notary's "certification" of such a copy may lend credibility to what is actually a counterfeit or altered document (*ARS* 41-311[3] and *ANPRM*).

Procedure. The Notary must make the photocopy of the original document to be certified. If the Notary does not have access to a photocopier, he or she cannot perform a copy certification. If a photocopier is available to the Notary, the Notary must first verify that the document presented is an original document. A copy certification cannot be performed on a copy of a document or on a certified copy. If the document presented is not an original, the Notary must refuse the notarization as a copy certification (*ARS* 41-311[3] and *ANPRM*).

ARIZONA NOTARY LAW PRIMER

Certificate for Certified Copy. The Notary must write or type on the face of the copied document the notarial language, as prescribed by the Secretary of State's office (*ANPRM*):

```
State of Arizona          )
                          )
County of _____       )


I, _____, a notary public, do certify that, on
the _____ day of _____[month], 20____, I personally
made the above/attached copy of _____ [title of document]
from the original, and it is a true, exact, complete, and unaltered copy.


[Seal]    _____ [Signature of Notary]
              Notary Public
```

Oaths and Affirmations

Purpose. An oath is a solemn, spoken pledge to a Supreme Being. An affirmation is a solemn, spoken pledge on one's own personal honor, with no reference to a Supreme Being. An individual who objects to taking an oath may instead take an affirmation. Both are usually a promise of truthfulness and have the same legal effect. In taking an oath or affirmation in an official proceeding, a person may be subject to criminal penalties for perjury should he or she fail to be truthful (*ARS* 41-311[10]).

An oath or affirmation can be a full-fledged notarial act in its own right, as when giving an oath of office to a public official ("swearing in" a public official), or it can be part of the process of notarizing a document (executing a jurat, swearing in a credible person).

Power to Administer. Arizona Notaries and certain other officers, such as judges and justices of the peace, are authorized to administer oaths and affirmations (*ARS* 33-501[1]).

Failure to Administer. Failing to administer any oath or affirmation as required by law could subject the Notary to charges of misconduct, which is grounds for the Secretary of State to deny, suspend or revoke a Notary's commission (*ARS* 41-330[A][9] and 41-368[A][9]).

Ceremony and Gestures. To impress upon the oath-taker or affirmant the importance of truthfulness, the Notary is encouraged to lend a sense of ceremony and formality to the oath or affirmation (*ARS* 12-2221). During administration of an oath or affirmation, the Notary and document signer traditionally raise their right hands, or their left ones, if for some reason the right hands cannot be raised, though this is not a legal requirement (*ANPRM*). Notaries generally have discretion to use words and gestures they feel will most compellingly appeal to the conscience of the oath-taker or affirmant.

Wording for Oath (Affirmation). The oath or affirmation wording must be spoken aloud by the Notary, and the person taking the oath or affirmation must answer aloud. A nod or grunt is not a clear and sufficient response. If a person is mute and unable to speak, the Notary may rely on written notes to communicate. An oath or affirmation may be read as either a statement or a question. The Notary asks the oath or affirmation taker either to repeat a statement after the Notary or to answer a question posed by the Notary. An Arizona Notary may use the following or similar words in administering an oath or affirmation to a signer or credible person (*ANPRM*):

1. For executing a jurat for a signer who is personally known to the Notary, a Notary may choose one of the following two forms:

    - "Please repeat the oath statement, by either swearing or affirming:

        'I, [insert signer's name], swear or affirm that the contents of this document are true and correct.'"

    OR

    - "Please answer the oath question with 'I do swear' or 'I do affirm':

        'Do you swear or affirm that the contents of this document are true and correct?'"

2. For swearing in a credible person identifying a signer for an acknowledgment, a Notary may choose one of the following two forms:

- "Please repeat the oath statement:

  'I, [insert credible person's name], swear or affirm that the person appearing before you and who signed this document is the person [he or she] claims to be.'"

  OR

- "Please answer the oath question with 'I do swear' or 'I do affirm':

  'Do you swear or affirm that the person appearing before me and who signed this document is the person [he/she] claims to be?'"

Jurats

Purpose. While the purpose of an acknowledgment is to positively identify a document signer, the purpose of a jurat is to compel truthfulness by appealing to the signer's conscience and fear of criminal penalties for perjury. A Notary normally executes a jurat in notarizing affidavits and other forms of written verification requiring an oath or affirmation by the signer, whenever the words "sworn to (or affirmed) before me," "subscribed and sworn to (or affirmed)" or similar phrases appear in the notarial language on the notarial certificate (*ANPRM*).

In executing a jurat, a Notary certifies that (*ARS* 41-311[6], 41-313[B][1] and 41-355[B][1]):

1) The signer personally appeared before the Notary at the time of notarization on the date and in the county indicated.

2) The signer was positively identified by the Notary through satisfactory evidence (See "Identifying Document Signers," page 44.).

3) The Notary administered an oath or affirmation to the signer.

4) The Notary witnessed the signature being made at the time of notarization.

Affidavits. An affidavit is a statement voluntarily signed and sworn to or affirmed before a Notary by a person called an affiant. Affidavits are used in and out of court for a variety of purposes, from declaring losses to an insurance company to declaring U.S. citizenship before traveling to a foreign country.

In order to notarize a signature on an affidavit, a Notary must administer an oath or affirmation and complete a jurat certificate. In an affidavit, the Notary's certificate typically sandwiches the affiant's signed statement, with the venue and affiant's name at the top of the document and the jurat wording at the end. The Notary is responsible for the venue, affiant's name and any notarial text at the beginning and end of the affidavit. The affiant is responsible for the signed statement in the middle.

Depositions. A deposition, or signed transcript of the signer's oral statements taken down for use in a judicial proceeding, also requires a jurat. Arizona Notaries do not have the power to take a deposition — that is, to write down the words of a witness (deponent) in a lawsuit or other official proceeding. However, Arizona Notaries may administer the oath or affirmation to a deponent who is about to give oral testimony that will be written down by another person, such as a shorthand or court reporter. In addition, Arizona Notaries may execute the jurat at the end of an already prepared deposition.

Foreign-Language Signatures. As of July 20, 2011, the signer whose signature is being notarized on a document containing a jurat must sign the document in a language the Notary understands. For example, a signer who wishes to sign in Chinese may do so only if the Notary also understands Chinese (*ARS* 41-313[B][2]).

Wording for Jurat Oaths (Affirmations). An Arizona Notary may use one of the following forms or similar wording to administer an oath (or affirmation) in conjunction with a jurat, remembering to require the person swearing (or affirming) to respond aloud (*ANPRM*):

- "Please repeat the oath statement, by either swearing or affirming:

    'I, [insert signer's name], swear or affirm that the contents of this document are true and correct.'"

    OR

- "Please answer the oath question with 'I do swear' or 'I do affirm':

    'Do you swear or affirm that the contents of this document are true and correct?'"

39

Failure to Administer Oath or Affirmation. Failing to administer any oath or affirmation as required by law could subject the Notary to charges of misconduct, which is grounds for the Secretary of State to deny, suspend or revoke a Notary's commission (*ARS* 41-330[A][9] and 41-368[A][9]).

Incomplete Documents. Because a signer is swearing/affirming that the information is true, a Notary may not perform a jurat on a document that is incomplete (*ARS* 41-328[A] and 41-366[A]).

Certificate for Jurat. The Secretary of State provides the following wording for a jurat (*ANPRM*):

    State of Arizona   )
)
    County of _____)

    Subscribed and sworn to (or affirmed) before me this _____ day of _____ [month], 20__.
    [Seal]   _____ [Signature of Notary]
                  Notary Public

Protests

Purpose. In rare instances, Notaries may be asked to protest a negotiable instrument for nonpayment. A protest is a written statement by a Notary or other authorized officer verifying that payment was not received on an instrument such as a bank draft. Failure to pay is called dishonor. Before issuing a certificate of protest, the Notary must present the bank draft or other instrument to the person or entity obliged to pay, a procedure called presentment. This act may be performed only by Notaries working as stockholders, directors, officers or employees of a corporation (*ARS* 41-320).

Antiquated Act. In the 19th century, protests were common notarial acts in the United States, but they rarely are performed today due to the advent of modern electronic communications and resulting changes in our banking and financial systems. Modern Notaries most often encounter protests in the context of international commerce.

Special Knowledge Required. Notarial acts of protest are complicated and varied, requiring a special knowledge of financial and legal terminology. Only Notaries who have the requisite special knowledge, or who are acting under the supervision of an experienced bank officer or an attorney familiar with the Uniform Commercial Code, should attempt to execute a protest.

PRACTICES AND PROCEDURES

Identifying Document Signers

Satisfactory Evidence. In taking acknowledgments and jurats for any document, Arizona law requires the Notary to identify the signer. The following three methods of identification are acceptable and considered satisfactory evidence of identity (*ARS* 41-311[11] and 41-351[14]):

1) The Notary's personal knowledge of the signer's identity (See "Personal Knowledge of Identity," below.)

2) Reliable identification documents or ID cards (See "Identification Documents," pages 42–44.)

3) The oath or affirmation of a credible person (See "Credible Person," pages 44–45.)

Identification for Other Notarial Acts. While the law specifies identification standards only for acknowledgments and jurats, the conscientious Notary will apply these same standards in identifying any signer for any official act.

Capacity of Signer. A person signing in a representative capacity, such as corporate officer, trustee, partner, attorney in fact or other capacity, must additionally acknowledge to the Notary that he or she does, in fact, have the authority to sign the document in the stated capacity. The Notary may ask for proof of authority to sign. A person signing as a corporate officer, for example, may be asked to present a copy of the corporation's articles of incorporation naming the officer (*ARS* 33-505).

Personal Knowledge of Identity

Definition. The safest and most reliable method of identifying a document signer is for the Notary to depend on his or her own personal knowledge of the signer's identity. Personal knowledge means familiarity with an individual resulting from interactions with that person over a period of time sufficient to eliminate reasonable doubt that the person has the identity claimed (*ARS* 41-311[10] and 41-351[13]). The familiarity should come from association with the individual in relation to other people and should be based upon a chain of circumstances surrounding the individual.

Arizona law does not specify how long a Notary must be acquainted with an individual before personal knowledge of identity may be claimed. The Notary's common sense must prevail. In general, the longer the Notary is acquainted with a person, and the more random interactions the Notary has had with that person in different situations and locations, the more likely the individual is indeed personally known. For instance, the Notary might safely regard a friend since childhood as personally known but would be foolish to consider a person met for the first time the previous day as such. Whenever the Notary has a reasonable doubt about a signer's identity, that individual should be considered not personally known, and the identification should be made through either a credible person or reliable identification documents.

Identification Documents (ID Cards)

Acceptable Identification Documents. Notaries Public and Electronic Notaries Public must accept only the following written forms of identification as proof of identity (*ARS* 41-311[11][a] and 41-351[14][a]):

1) An unexpired driver license that is issued by a state or territory of the United States

2) An unexpired passport that is issued by the United States Department of State

3) An unexpired identification card that is issued by any branch of the United States Armed Forces

4) Any other unexpired identification card that is issued by the United States government or a state or tribal government that contains the individual's photograph, signature and physical description consisting of the individual's height, weight, color of hair and color of eyes

Identification Documents for Real Estate Transactions. In addition to the acceptable forms of written identification listed above, for the purposes of real estate conveyance or financing, a person's identity may be proved by one of the following (*ARS* 41-311[11][b] and 41-351[14][b]):

1) A valid unexpired passport that is issued by a national government other than the United States government, accompanied by a valid unexpired visa or other documentation that is issued by the United States government and which is necessary to establish an individual's legal presence in the United States

2) Any other valid unexpired identification that is accepted by the United States Department of Homeland Security to establish an individual's legal presence in the United States, accompanied by supporting documents as required by the United States Department of Homeland Security

Multiple Identification Documents. While one acceptable identification document or card may be sufficient to identify a signer, the Notary may ask for more. At least one ID card must satisfy all of the above criteria, however.

Unacceptable Identification Documents. Unacceptable ID cards for identifying signers include Social Security cards, credit cards, voter registration cards or identification cards issued by private employers.

Fraudulent Identification Documents. Identification documents are the least secure of the three methods of identifying a document signer because phony ID cards are common. The Notary should scrutinize each card for evidence of tampering or counterfeiting, or for evidence that it is a genuine card that has been issued to an impostor.

Some clues that an ID card may have been fraudulently tampered with include mismatched type styles, a photograph that is raised from the surface, a signature that does not match the signature on the document, unauthorized lamination of the card and smudges, erasures, smears and discolorations.

Possible tip-offs to a counterfeit ID card include misspelled words, a brand-new-looking card with an old date of issuance, two cards with exactly the same photograph and inappropriate patterns and textures.

Some possible indications that a card may have been issued to an impostor are that the card's birth date or address is unknown to the bearer, all of the individual's ID cards seem brand new and the bearer is unwilling to leave a thumbprint in the journal. (Such a print is not a legal requirement but is requested by some Notaries as protection against forgers and lawsuits. Refusal to leave a thumbprint is not in itself grounds to deny a notarization.)

Credible Person

Purpose. When a document signer is not personally known to the Notary and is not able to present reliable ID cards, that signer may be identified on the oath (or affirmation) of a credible person who personally knows the document signer. In a sense, a credible person is a walking, talking ID card. Credible persons are sometimes called "credible identifying witnesses" or "credible witnesses" (*ARS* 41-311[11][a][v] and [vi], 41-351[14][a][v] and [vi], and *ANPRM*).

Qualifications. There are two types of credible persons. The first is a person whom the Notary knows. In this case, the satisfactory evidence of the credible person's identity is the Notary's personal knowledge, resulting in the establishment of a chain of personal knowledge from the Notary through the credible identifying witness to the signer (*ARS* 41-311[11][a] and 41-351[14][a]). The second type of credible person is one whom the Notary does not know. This credible person must present a valid ID card that will serve as satisfactory evidence of identity (*ARS* 41-311[11][a] and 41-351[14][a]). (See "Identification Documents," pages 42–44.)

Both types of credible persons must personally know the document signer. In addition, any credible person should appear to the Notary to understand the role of a credible person, and have a reputation for honesty and integrity. The credible person should be a competent individual who won't be tricked, cajoled, bullied or otherwise influenced into identifying someone he or she does not really know. Finally, a credible person should have no financial interest in the transaction and should not be named in the document.

Oaths (Affirmations) for Credible Person. To ensure truthfulness, the Notary must administer an oath or affirmation to each credible person. According to the Secretary of State's office, the following is an acceptable oath (or affirmation) (*ANPRM*):

- "Please repeat the oath statement:

  'I, [insert credible person's name], swear or affirm that the person appearing before you and who signed this document is the person [he or she] claims to be.'"

OR

- "Please answer the oath question with 'I do swear' or 'I do affirm':

  'Do you swear or affirm that the person appearing before me and who signed this document is the person [he or she] claims to be?'"

<u>Signature in Notary's Journal</u>. Each credible person must sign the Notary's journal, as must the document signer. The Notary also must enter the method by which the credible person was identified, either by personal knowledge or an ID card (*ANPRM*). The National Notary Association recommends that the Notary also print the credible person's name and address in the journal.

Journal of Notarial Acts

<u>Requirement</u>. A journal provides proof that a Notary Public performed a notarization and verifies that the Notary took reasonable steps to identify the signer of a document. Arizona Notaries are required to keep a chronological paper journal of all their official acts. The journal entry is to be made at the time of notarization — never later. The journal should be in the form of a permanently bound record book (not loose-leaf). Journals that contain consecutively numbered pages and entry spaces are best for preserving the sequence of notarial acts and for protecting against unauthorized removal of pages or tampering (*ARS* 41-313, 41-319[A], 41-355[D], 41-361[A] and *ANPRM*).

<u>Public vs. Private Journal</u>. A Notary may keep two official journals: one to list all public acts and one to list all acts that are protected by attorney-client privilege or that are confidential due to state or federal law. Many Notaries keep only a public-records journal because they do not perform notarizations on any nonpublic documents. If Notaries perform only public-record notarizations, they may not keep one journal at home and one at the office (*ARS* 41-319[A], 41-361[A] and *ANPRM*).

ARIZONA NOTARY LAW PRIMER

Court Reporters' Journals. Non-Notary court reporters who administer oaths and affirmations in judicial proceedings are not required to maintain a record of such acts. However, court reporters who are also commissioned Notaries and perform notarial acts outside of judicial proceedings are subject to all of the provisions of the Arizona Notary Public laws, including the requirement of maintaining a journal for all notarial acts (*ARS* 41-324[A]). The only exception is that court reporters who administer oaths or affirmations in judicial proceedings are not required to obtain signatures in their journals (*ARS* 41-324[B]).

Alternative Records. If a Notary personally knows a signer, the Notary may satisfy the statutory recordkeeping requirements by retaining a paper or electronic copy of the notarized document in lieu of a journal entry (*ARS* 41-319[B] and 41-361[B]).

Journal Entries. A Notary is required to make a separate journal entry for each notarization that must contain at least the following entries (*ARS* 41-319[A] and 41-361[A]):

1) The date the notarization was performed

2) The type of notarization (jurat, acknowledgment, etc.) or description of the document (Deed of Trust, Affidavit of Support, Power of Attorney, etc.)

3) The signature, full printed name and address of each signer

4) A statement of how the signer was identified (If by personal knowledge, the journal notation would read "Personal Knowledge." If by a credible person, the notation would be "Credible Person," followed by the person's name, method by which the credible person was identified and the credible person's signature. If by an identification document, the following would be recorded: type of ID and its issuing agency, serial or identification number, and date of issuance or expiration.)

5) The fee charged, if any, for the notarial service

Additional Entries. Notaries may include additional information in their journals that is pertinent to a given notarization. For

NOTARY LAWS EXPLAINED

instance, while only the type of notarization or the description of the document is required by law, the Secretary of State recommends that a Notary fill in both fields if they are offered in the journal (*ANPRM.*). Another important entry to include is the signer's representative capacity if not signing on his or her own behalf — whether attorney in fact, trustee, guardian, corporate officer or other capacity. Many Notaries also enter telephone numbers of every signer and witness, as well as the address where the notarization was performed, if not at the Notary's office. Including the time of day of the notarization is helpful when recalling a notarization. A description of the document signer's demeanor ("The signer appeared very nervous.") or notations about the identity of other persons who were present for the notarization also may be pertinent.

If a Notary refuses a notarization for any reason, the Notary should always make a notation in his or her journal about the refusal and the grounds for doing so in case legal action ensues. There is no guarantee that a journal entry will exonerate a Notary, but a Notary should be in the habit of documenting the reason for the refusal (*ANPRM*).

Multiple Notarizations for the Same Individual. If a Notary performs more than one notarization for an individual within one six-month period, the Notary must obtain satisfactory evidence of identity and a journal signature for the first notarization, but may not require identification or a journal signature for second and subsequent notarizations within the same six-month period (*ARS* 41-319[C] and 41-361[C]). However, nothing prevents a Notary from asking for current identification and a journal signature for each and every notarial act, even though identification and a signature by the individual cannot be required for signers in this case.

If a Notary performs more than one notarization of the same type for a signer either on like documents or within the same document and at the same time, the Notary may group the documents together and make one journal entry for the transaction (*ARS* 41-319[D] and 41-361[D]).

Journal Thumbprint. Increasingly, Notaries are asking document signers to leave a thumbprint in the journal. The journal thumbprint is a strong deterrent against forgery because it represents absolute proof of the forger's identity. While it cannot be made a precondition for notarizing, nothing prevents a Notary from asking for a thumbprint for every notarial act, if the signer is willing (*ANPRM*).

Inspection or Certified Copies of Journal Entry. A Notary's journal of notarial acts is a public record. Accordingly, a Notary must comply with anyone's request to inspect an entry in the journal, and must provide a certified copy of any journal entry or other notarial record — except if the record is confidential due to state or federal law or attorney-client privilege (*ARS* 41-319[A] and *ANPRM*).

However, the requesting individual must submit a written request specifying the month and year of a particular notarization, the type of document and the names of the signers (*ARS* 41-319[F] and 41-361[D]). Upon receipt of this notice, the Notary may provide that person with a certified copy of the particular entry in the journal, but of no other entries. Adjacent entries may be covered by a sheet of blank paper. If the person who makes the request has not done so in writing or cannot supply the requested information, the Notary may refuse the request. The Notary may charge no more than $2 per photocopy certified (*ARS* 41-316, 41-319 and *AAC* R2-12-1102).

Certificate for Certified Copy of Notarial Record. The National Notary Association recommends using the following or a similar certificate in certifying a copy of an entry or page from the Notary's official journal:

State of Arizona   )
)
County of _____   )

On this _____ day of _____ [month], _____ [year], I hereby certify that the attached is a complete, true, and accurate photocopy of a/an page/entry in my official Notary Journal, requested by and presented/mailed to _____ [name of recipient] on this day.

[Seal]   _____ [Signature of Notary]
Notary Public

Control of Journal. Notaries should never surrender control of their official journal of public records to anyone. Even when an employer has paid for the Notary's official journal and seal, they go with the Notary upon termination of employment. No person but the Notary can lawfully possess and use them.

However, a Notary's journal of nonpublic acts belongs to the employer, and the Notary must surrender it to the employer upon termination of employment (ARS 41-319[E] and ANPRM).

Lost or Stolen Journal. The Secretary of State requires notification by certified mail or other means that provides a receipt of delivery within 10 days if a journal is lost or stolen. In the notification, the Notary must sign a notice of loss or theft. Any person who fails to notify the Secretary of State's office within 30 days of the loss is subject to a $25 civil penalty in addition to possible suspension or revocation of the Notary's commission for failure of duty. In the case of a stolen journal, the Notary is obligated to inform the appropriate law enforcement agency. (*ARS* 41-323, 41-364[B] and *ANPRM*).

A Notary should replace his or her journal if it is lost or stolen. The Secretary of State recommends that the Notary explain in the replacement journal why it is being used (*ARS* 41-323[B] and *ANPRM*).

Storage of Notarial Records. All commissioned Notaries are required to securely store their records for five years from the date of notarization (*ARS* 41-317[B] and 41-359[B]). After that, they may destroy the records.

Destruction of Notarial Records. Any person who knowingly destroys, defaces or conceals a Notary's journal, journal entry or any other records belonging to the office of a Notary Public may be fined up to $500. A person who does so is also liable for damages to any party injured by such actions (*ARS* 41-318).

Disposal of Notary Records. If a Notary resigns, is removed from office or does not renew his or her commission, then his or her notarial records must be delivered to the Secretary of State's office as soon as the commission is surrendered by certified mail or other means of providing a receipt. Surrendered journals should have entries that are no more than five years old. If the journal has information that is more than five years old, the journal should be destroyed by the Notary or his or her representative. If a Notary neglects to turn in his or her records within three months, the Notary may be fined $50 to $500 (*ARS* 41-317[A] and *ANPRM*).

ARIZONA NOTARY LAW PRIMER

If the Notary dies, the Notary's heirs or personal representative also must surrender the Notary's records within three months of his or her appointment as the Notary's representative. If the personal representative neglects to turn in the Notary's records within three months, the representative may be fined $50 to $500 (*ARS* 41-317[A]).

The Secretary of State's office will keep all notarial records on file for five years and will give certified copies when requested. (*ARS* 41-317[B] and *ANPRM*).

Notarial Certificate

Requirement. In notarizing any document, a Notary must complete a notarial certificate. The certificate is wording that indicates exactly what the Notary is attesting (*ARS* 41-311[8]). If a Notary fails to complete notarial wording for a notarization on a document, the Notary may have his or her commission revoked (*ARS* 41-330[8]) and a court may consider the notarization invalid (*ANPRM*). The notarial certificate may be either on the document itself or on an attachment to it. The certificate should contain:

1) A *venue* indicating the state and county where the notarization is being performed, not necessarily where the Notary's commission is filed, where the Notary's business is located or where the Notary or the signer resides (*ARS* 41-311[12]). "State of Arizona, County of _____," is the typical venue wording, with the county name inserted in the blank. In some cases, both state and county names are preprinted on the certificate; in others, the Notary needs to fill them in. The letters "SS." or "SCT." sometimes appear after the venue. They abbreviate the Latin word *scilicet*, meaning "in particular" or "namely."

2) A *statement of particulars*, the text that indicates to what the Notary is attesting in a particular notarization. An acknowledgment certificate would include such wording as: "On this _____ day of _____ (month), _____ (year), before me personally appeared, _____ whom I know personally, and acknowledged that he/she executed the above document." A jurat certificate would include such wording as: "Subscribed and sworn to (or affirmed) before me this _____ day of _____ (month), _____ (year) by _____ (name of signer)." The Notary should fill in

the blanks with the appropriate date, his or her own name, the name(s) of the signer(s) and any other information required for that particular certificate.

3) A *testimonium clause*, by which the Notary formally attests to the truthfulness of the preceding facts in the certificate. A testimonium clause may appear if the date is not included in the statement of particulars. This clause typically reads: "Witness my hand and official seal, this the _____ day of _____ (month), _____ (year)." The Notary's "hand" or signature follows the testimonium clause, along with the imprint of the Notary's seal. This clause is sometimes omitted because the Notary's act of affixing a signature and seal to the certificate serves as sufficient confirmation of the facts in the certificate.

4) The *official signature of the Notary*, exactly as it appears on the Notary's application and commission. The official signature of the Notary must be made by hand at the time of the notarization. A Notary should not use a rubber signature stamp. A Notary should place his or her signature near — above or next to — the title "Notary Public." It is essential that the Notary who performs the notarization must be clearly identified by the title of "Notary Public," which may be printed on the certificate (*ANPRM*).

5) The *official seal of the Notary*. On many certificates, the letters "L.S." appear, indicating where the seal impression is to be placed. These letters abbreviate the Latin term *locus sigilli*, meaning "location of the seal." The ink seal impression should be placed near but not over the letters. Only an embossing seal, when used with an inking seal stamp, may be placed directly over these letters.

<u>Language of Notarial Certificate</u>. As of July 20, 2011, a notarial certificate signed by a Notary must be worded and completed using only letters, characters and a language the Notary can read, write and understand (*ARS* 41-313[B][4] and 41-355[B][4]).

<u>Commission Expiration Date</u>. Notaries are no longer required to write the date of their commission expiration separately on documents on which they execute a notarial act (*ARS* 41-313[B][3]).

It is sufficient that a Notary's seal contains his or her commission expiration date. If a space for the commission expiration date is provided, however, a Notary should fill it in (*ANPRM*).

Correcting Certificates. If any part of the notarial certificate is incorrect, the Notary should either cross out the incorrect words with ink or cross out the entire wording and type or write in the correct wording. A Notary should not attempt to erase words or use correction fluid or tape, and must be sure to initial any changes (*ANPRM*). If an error is discovered after the time of notarization, a person may correct a notarial certificate if that person brings action in the superior court to obtain a judgment for correction (*ARS* 33-513).

Loose Certificates. When certificate wording is not preprinted on the document for the Notary to fill out, a "loose" certificate may be attached. The Notary must ask the person requesting the notarization which type of notarization he or she wants. Once this is determined, the Notary can type or neatly handwrite this information on the document or attach a certificate on a separate piece of paper.

A Notary should also use a loose certificate when there is not enough room on the document for both certificate wording (preprinted or not) and the Notary's signature and seal, or in instances when the preprinted wording does not substantially agree with wording that is legal in Arizona. It is best to place the notarial certificate, signature and official seal on the same page as the signatures being witnessed or acknowledged to make it unlikely that the certificate could be fraudulently attached to another document (*ANPRM*).

Normally, a loose certificate is stapled to the document's left margin following the signature page. Only one side of the certificate should be stapled.

As of July 20, 2011, any "loose" certificate completed by a Notary must contain the following description of the document to which it is attached (ARS 41-313[C] and 4-355[C]):

- The title or type of document;

- The document date;

- The number of pages; and

- The names of any additional signers not named in the notarial certificate.

To prevent a loose certificate from being removed and fraudulently placed on another document, a Notary can take certain precautions. The Notary can emboss the certificate and document together, writing "Attached document bears embossment" on the certificate.

While fraud-deterrent steps such as the above can make it much more difficult for a loose certificate to be removed and misused, there is no absolute protection against its removal and misuse. While a loose certificate remains in their control, however, Notaries must absolutely ensure that the certificate is attached only to its intended document. Notaries must never permit other persons to attach loose notarial certificates to documents.

Do Not Pre-Sign/Seal Certificates. A Notary should never sign and/or seal certificates ahead of the time of notarization. Nor should the Notary send an unattached, signed and sealed loose certificate through the mail, even if requested to do so by a signer who previously appeared before the Notary with a document. These actions may facilitate fraud or forgery, and they could subject the Notary to lawsuits to recover damages resulting from the Notary's negligence or misconduct.

Size for Certificates. Arizona county recorders will not accept documents for recording, including notarial certificates, that do not comply with the following requirements (*ARS* 11-480):

1) Printing must be 10-point type or larger.

2) Margins must be at least one-half inch at the top, bottom and sides, with two inches left at the top of the first page. These margins must contain no print, writing, seals or other markings.

3) No document pages may be larger than 8½ inches in width and 14 inches in length.

False Certificate. A Notary who completes a notarial certificate containing statements that the Notary is sure are false is guilty of a Class 6 Felony and is subject to criminal penalties. In addition, the Secretary of State may deny, suspend or revoke the Notary's commission. A Notary would be completing a false certificate,

ARIZONA NOTARY LAW PRIMER

for example, if he or she signed and sealed an acknowledgment certificate indicating that a signer personally appeared when the signer did not. (*ARS* 38-423, 39-161, 41-330[A][10] and *ANPRM*).

Notary Seal

Requirement. An Arizona Notary must affix an impression of his or her official seal on the certificate portion of every document notarized (*ARS* 41-313[B]). Although the Arizona Attorney General has stated that short-form certificates of acknowledgment do not require authentication with a Notary seal, recorders generally will not accept any certificates without a seal impression.

Purchase of Seal. No person may purchase an Arizona Notary seal without first presenting to the seal vendor a photocopy of the Notary commission certificate. It is a Class 3 Misdemeanor for a person, firm or agency to make, manufacture or otherwise produce an Arizona Notary seal without retaining a photocopy of the Notary's commission. The seal vendor must retain the commission certificate copy on file for four years (ARS 41-321).

Seal Format. The inking rubber stamp makes the official Arizona Notary seal impression. The stamp must imprint a photographically reproducible impression in dark ink — the Secretary of State suggests black, dark brown, dark blue, dark green or purple. An embosser may be used in addition to the required inking stamp, but cannot serve as the Notary's only seal. An embossment must not be placed over the inked seal impression or the Notary's signature (*ARS* 41-313 and *ANPRM*).

State law prescribes that Arizona Notaries must use an inking rubber stamp that imprints an image no larger than 1½ inches high by 2½ inches wide. Arizona does not have a shape requirement; however, most inking stamp seals traditionally are rectangular, since a rectangular impression takes up less document space than a circular one. Rectangular stamp impressions may even be placed lengthwise in a document's margin if no other space is available (*ARS* 41-313 and 41-321[B]).

Seal Components. The seal impression must clearly show the following information (*ARS* 41-313[B][2]):

- The name of the Notary exactly as it appears on the Notary's commission application

- The words "Notary Public"

- The name of the county in which the Notary is commissioned

- The Notary's commission expiration date

- The Great Seal of the State of Arizona

Placement of Seal Impression. The Notary's official seal impression should be placed near (but not over) the Notary's signature on the notarial certificate and must be easily readable. The Secretary of State suggests that the seal impression be placed below and to the left of the certificate wording (*ANPRM*).

Whenever possible — and especially on documents that will be submitted to a public recorder — the Notary should avoid affixing the seal over any text or signatures on the document or certificate. Some recorders will reject documents if writing or document text intrudes within the borders the Notary's seal impression. If the document leaves no room for the seal impression, the Notary may have no choice but to complete and attach a loose certificate that duplicates the notarial wording from the document. With documents that will not be publicly recorded, however, the recipient may allow the Notary to stamp the seal over boilerplate text —standard clauses or sections of the document — as long as the wording within the seal impression is not obscured (*ANPRM*).

L.S. The letters "L.S." — from the Latin *locus sigilli*, meaning "location of the seal" — appear on many notarial certificates to indicate where the Notary seal impression should be placed. Only an embosser seal, used in addition to an inking stamp seal, should be placed over these letters. The ink seal impression should be placed near but not over the letters.

Lost or Stolen Seal. Any Notary whose official seal stamp is lost or stolen must, within 10 days, notify the Secretary of State in writing by certified mail or other means that provides a receipt. In the case of theft, the Notary must also inform the appropriate law enforcement agency. Failure to report a lost or stolen seal will subject the Notary to a $25 civil penalty. Also, the Secretary of State may deny, suspend or revoke the Notary's commission for failure of duty (*ARS* 41-323[B]).

Replacing a Notary Seal. A Notary should replace a lost or stolen seal stamp. The shape and ink color of the replacement stamp should be different than the original one, although the replacement seal stamp should be no more than 1½ inches high and 2½ inches long, as required by statute (*ARS* 41- 321[B]). Once the Notary receives the new seal stamp, he or she must describe the replacement stamp to the law enforcement agency to which he or she reported the theft of the original seal stamp. The Notary should also contact the Secretary of State's office in writing with the description of the new seal stamp, and document in his or her journal the date when he or she started to use the replacement seal stamp (*ANPRM*).

Disposition of Seal. When a Notary resigns a commission, has a commission revoked, allows a commission to expire and does not intend to renew it, or dies while in office, the Notary or the Notary's representative must deliver his or her seal stamp to the Secretary of State's office (*ARS* 41-317[A]). A Notary who resigns a commission but later is granted a new commission must purchase a new seal stamp with the new expiration date on it before performing a notarization (*ANPRM*).

Fees for Notarial Services

Must Post Fee Schedule. Every Arizona Notary is required to post in a conspicuous place in his or her office a complete table of the fees which Notaries are allowed to charge. This fee schedule must remain posted at all times. Printing the fees in a brochure is not considered a "conspicuous" posting (*ARS* 38-412 and *ANPRM*).

Authorized Fees. A Notary may only advertise or charge a fee for performing a notarial act that is specifically authorized by the Secretary of State in administrative rule (*ARS* 41-316[C]). Arizona Administrative Code Section R2-12-1102 and R2-12-1207 contain the maximum fees a Notary may advertise or charge.

- Acknowledgments. For taking an acknowledgment, the fee is not to exceed $2 for each signature notarized ($25 for an electronic acknowledgment). For notarizing three signatures on a single document, for example, a maximum of $6 could be charged (or $75 for an electronic acknowledgment).

- Copy Certifications. A maximum of $2 per page may be charged by a Notary for providing a certified copy.

- Oaths and Affirmations. For administering an oath or affirmation without a signature, the maximum fee is $2 ($25 for electronic Notaries).

- Jurats. For executing a jurat, including the administration of the oath or affirmation, the fee is not to exceed $2 per signature ($25 for electronic jurats).

- Protests — Not listed. For executing a protest, the law is silent on how much can be charged. Since only certain Notaries may execute protests, it is likely that they would not charge because it would be considered part of their jobs.

Charging for Certain Acts Prohibited. No fee is allowed for taking an acknowledgment for a claim for a federal pension, allotment, allowance, compensation, insurance or other benefits. Any Notary who violates this provision is liable upon his or her bond (*ARS* 39-122).

Neither is any fee is allowed for the administration of any oath or affirmation required in the military (*ARS* 26-160).

Option Not to Charge. Notaries are not required to charge for their notarial services, and they may charge any fee less than the maximum. But a Notary's fees must be "set and consistent." That is, a Notary should charge the same fee each time he or she notarizes (*ANPRM*). Laws prohibiting discrimination may apply to the Notary's practice of charging fees and can provide the basis for lawsuits. Discrimination against anyone who presents a lawful request for notarization simply is not a suitable policy for a public official appointed to serve all of the public equally (*ANPRM*).

Because Arizona statute does not regulate whether or to whom a Notary charges a fee, such decisions may be negotiated between a Notary and his or her employer. Companies and organizations that employ Notaries can request them to charge the fees as set in the Notary fees schedule. If a public or private entity employs a Notary, the fees charged during normal work hours are the property of the employer (*ANPRM*).

ARIZONA NOTARY LAW PRIMER

Overcharging Prohibited. A Notary may not charge a service or transaction fee in addition to the fee for notarization. Companies and organizations that employ Notaries may not ask them to charge more than the $2 fee. Charging more than the legally prescribed fee is a Class 5 Felony. If a Notary charges a higher fee than prescribed by rule, or any fee not allowed, then the Notary will be liable to the overcharged party for four times the amount unlawfully demanded and received and the Secretary of State may deny, suspend or revoke the commission (*ARS* 38-413 and 41-330[A][6] and *ANPRM*).

Travel Fees. Notaries may charge a mileage fee and a per diem if travel is necessary, but the Notary may not charge more than the amount allowed state employees (*ARS* 38-413). The Arizona Department of Administration sets the mileage fee and posts the fee schedule at www.agao.az.gov/travel. A Notary Public who plans to charge this fee should contact the Department of Administration's General Accounting Office to make sure that this mileage fee is current (*ANPRM*).

The National Notary Association recommends that before the Notary travels, the Notary and signer agree on a fee, and that the Notary tell the signer that these travel fees are separate from the notarial fees.

Refusal of Services

Legal Requests. Notaries must honor all lawful and reasonable requests to notarize, whether or not the person requesting the act is a client or customer of the Notary or the Notary's employer. An employer of a Notary Public may not limit the Notary's services to customers or other persons designated by that employer (*ARS* 41-312[C][3]). Not providing services when required to do so could cause the Notary to be liable if any damages resulted from the refusal (*ANPRM*).

Business Hours. Notaries are not expected to be available to notarize for the public other than during the Notary's normal business hours. However, a Notary may choose to offer notarial services at any hour. An employer may not prohibit the Notary from notarizing away from work, even if the employer paid for the Notary's commission and supplies (*ANPRM*).

Grounds for Refusing Service. A Notary should refuse to notarize, however, if any of the following situations exist (*ANPRM*):

- the signer is not present

- the Notary doesn't believe the signer understands what he or she is signing

- it appears that the signer is not signing willingly

- the signer cannot present satisfactory identification

- the Notary believes the identification presented is fraudulent

- the document signatures are not original

- the document has blanks or is not complete

- there is no notarial wording and the signer doesn't know what type of notarization should be performed

- the document is written in a language that the Notary does not have a general understanding of

- a request for a copy of a journal entry is not made in writing

- the Notary does not have access to a photocopy machine when a copy certification is requested

- a person presents a public or publicly recordable document for copy certification

Signature by Mark

Mark Serves as Signature. A person who cannot sign his or her name because of illiteracy or a physical disability may instead use a mark — an "X" or a thumbprint, for example — as a signature, as long as there is a witness to the making of the mark (*ANPRM*).

Witness. In order for the mark to be a fully legal signature, it must be properly witnessed. A person in addition to the Notary must witness the signing by mark. The witness must then print the marker's name beside the mark (and also in the journal) and sign the document and the Notary's journal as a witness (e.g., "John Q. Smith, Witness"). The Notary witnesses both the making of the mark and the witness's writing the signer's name, and notarizes both signatures (*ANPRM*).

A witness is not required if the Notary personally knows the marker or if the Notary can identify the marker through sufficient identification documents. In this case, the Notary serves as the sole witness and must write the marker's name beside the mark. However, if the marker needs a credible person to prove identity to the Notary, the credible person acts as the witness and writes the marker's name (*ARS* 1-215[37] and *ANPRM*).

Notarizing for Minors

Under Age 18. Generally, persons must reach the age of majority before they can handle their own legal affairs and sign documents for themselves. In Arizona, the age of majority is 18. Normally, parents or court-appointed guardians will sign on a minor's behalf. In certain cases, minors who are engaged in business transactions or children serving as court witnesses may lawfully sign documents and have their signatures notarized.

Identification. The method for identifying a minor is the same as for an adult. However, determining the identity of a minor can be a problem because minors often do not possess acceptable identification documents such as driver's licenses. If the minor does not have acceptable ID, then one of the other methods of identifying acknowledgers must be used, either the Notary's personal knowledge of the minor or the oath of a credible person who can identify the minor. (See "Credible Person," pages 44–45.)

Include Age Next to Signature. When notarizing for a minor, the Notary should ask the young signer to write his or her age next to the signature to alert any person relying on the document that the signer is a minor. The Notary is not required to verify the minor signer's age.

Disqualifying Interest

Impartiality. Notaries are appointed by the state to be impartial, disinterested witnesses whose screening duties help ensure the integrity of important legal and commercial transactions. Lack of impartiality by a Notary throws doubt on the integrity and lawfulness of any transaction.

A Notary may not notarize a signature on a document if any of the following apply (*ARS* 41-328[C] and 41-366[C]):

- The signature is the Notary's

- The Notary is a party to the document

- The Notary is an officer of any named party to the document

- The Notary will receive any direct material benefit from the transaction that exceeds in value the fees for the notarial act authorized by *ARS* Section 41-316

Direct Material Benefit. A direct material benefit exists when the Notary receives an advantage, right, privilege, property or fee valued in excess of the lawfully prescribed notarial fee.

Exceptions. A Notary who is a stockholder, director, officer or employee of a corporation is permitted to notarize a document affecting the corporation, unless the Notary is a party to the document, either individually or as a corporate representative (*ARS* 41-320 and 41-362).

Relatives. Arizona law states that a Notary may not notarize for anyone related by marriage or adoption (*ARS* 41-328[C] and 41-366[C]). While this means a Notary could notarize for someone related by blood, such as a sibling, Notaries who do so may endanger their status as impartial witnesses and violate the statutes prohibiting a direct material benefit. The Secretary of State recommends that a Notary never notarize the signature of any close family member in order to avoid any misunderstandings or problems of interpretation of interests (*ANPRM*).

Unauthorized Practice of Law

Advice or Assistance Prohibited. Notaries are ministerial officials who follow simple, written rules without applying significant judgment or discretion. Notaries who are not attorneys may not give legal advice or accept fees for legal advice, and should not assist other persons in drafting, preparing, selecting, completing or understanding a document or transaction.
This means that a Notary should not fill in the blanks in a document for others, tell others what document they need in a given instance or how to draft it, or advise others about the legal sufficiency of a document — and especially not for a fee (*ANPRM*). Notaries who overstep their authority by advising others on legal matters may have their commissions revoked and may be prosecuted for the unauthorized practice of law.

As a private individual, a Notary may prepare legal documents to which he or she is personally a party; but the Notary may not then notarize his or her signature on these documents.

Wills

Advice or Assistance Prohibited. People often attempt to draw up wills on their own without the benefit of legal counsel and then bring these homemade testaments to a Notary to have them "legalized," expecting the Notary to know how to proceed. But wills are complex documents, whose format is strictly dictated by law. The slightest deviation from these laws can nullify a will. Unless a Notary is working at the direction of an attorney, who has provided clear instructions and a notarial certificate for each signer, or unless the Notary has had extensive estate planning experience, he or she should avoid notarizing signatures on a will.

Even if the Notary has had estate-planning experience, he or she should avoid giving advice about a will unless he or she is an attorney. Any questions the signers ask about how to proceed must be answered by an attorney. In advising or assisting people who bring wills for notarization, the Notary risks prosecution for the unauthorized practice of law. The Notary's ill-informed advice may do considerable damage to the affairs of the signer and subject the Notary to a lawsuit to recover losses.

Living Wills. Documents popularly called living wills may be notarized. These are not actual wills, but a form of advance health care directive in which the signer gives written instructions for medical treatment in the event that he or she later becomes unable to provide such instructions due to illness or incapacity.

Advertising

False or Misleading Advertising. A Notary's commission can be revoked or suspended if the Notary uses false or misleading advertising to misrepresent the qualifications, powers, duties, rights or privileges of a Notary. A Notary may also be liable in a civil lawsuit if it is determined that the Notary's misrepresentation of his or her powers caused a party financial damage. Furthermore, the Secretary of State may deny, suspend or revoke a Notary's commission (*ARS* 41-329, 41-330[A][5] and *ANPRM*).

A Notary should not use the terms *Notario, Notario Publico* or an equivalent non-English term for advertisements, notices, business cards, stationery and signage, because such terms may imply to those unfamiliar with the limited powers of U.S. Notaries that legal services are being provided. Instead, a Notary should use only the commission title "Notary Public" (*ANPRM*).

A nonattorney Notary who advertises notarial services in a language other than English, by means of any form of communication other than a single desk plaque, should prominently display this statement in the same language: "I am not an attorney and cannot give legal advice about immigration or any other legal matters." Failure to post this statement in any ad is a Class 6 Felony, and the Notary's commission shall be permanently revoked (*ARS* 41-329).

Advertising Unauthorized Fee. A Notary may not advertise a fee for a notarial act that is not specifically authorized by the Secretary of State in administrative rule (*ARS* 41-316[C] and 41-358[C], and *AAC* R2-12-1102 and R2-12-1207).

Foreign Languages

Foreign-Language Documents. Although Arizona Notaries are not prohibited from notarizing a signature on a document written in a language the Notary cannot read, there are difficulties and dangers in notarizing a signature on a document and completing a certificate written in a language the Notary cannot read.

First, if the Notary cannot read the certificate, he or she may be unable to determine what type of notarial act is required, may fail to comply with instructions given in the certificate wording (e.g., to administer an oath) or may unwittingly attest to actions outside the scope of his or her authority. Even when the Notary can read the certificate wording, it will be difficult to extract information from a document that the Notary cannot read in order to enter it in the journal. But the foremost danger to notarizing a signature on a document written in a language the Notary cannot read is that the document may be misrepresented. Although Notaries are not required to read the documents they notarize, when extracting data for their journals and completing certificates they sometimes cannot help but notice that a document is fraudulent. It is nearly impossible for a Notary to detect a fraud when the document is in a language the Notary cannot understand.

As an alternative to performing the notarization in such a situation, the Notary may refer the signer to another Notary Public who is able to read the language in which the document is written, or to a relevant foreign consulate. Many foreign countries have consulates in certain major U.S. cities, and most consulates have staff members with notarial powers.

Foreign-Language Signatures. Effective July 20, 2011, the signer whose signature is being notarized on a document must sign the document in a language the Notary understands. (*ARS* 41-313[B][2] and 41-355[B][2]).

Foreign-Language Certificates. Effective July 20, 2011, a notarial certificate signed by a Notary must be worded and completed using only letters, characters and a language the Notary can read, write and understand (*ARS* 41-313[B][4] and 41-355[B][4]).

Foreign-Language Speakers. An Arizona Notary may perform a notarial act for a document signer with whom the Notary can directly or indirectly communicate. When the Notary and signer speak the same language, the Notary may proceed with the notarization following all rules for performing notarial acts as discussed in this *Primer*.

When the Notary and signer do not speak the same language, Arizona statute now authorizes the Notary and signer to indirectly communicate through a translator. The translator must be physically present with the Notary and signer at the time the notarization is performed and be able to directly communicate with the Notary and signer in languages the translator understands (*ARS* 41-313[B][3] and 41-355[B][3]).

Immigration Documents

Advice or Assistance Prohibited. A Notary Public should not claim to have powers, qualifications, rights or privileges that the office of Notary does not provide, including the qualification to counsel on the subject of immigration. Anyone who is not an attorney may never advise others on immigration matters or help others to prepare immigration documents — and especially not for a fee. Notaries who offer immigration advice or assistance to others may be prosecuted for the unauthorized practice of law.

Notarizing Immigration Documents. While Notaries may not offer advice on immigration matters, they may notarize immigration documents. Of the forms issued or accepted by the U.S. Citizenship and Immigration Services (USCIS), affidavits are the ones most often presented for notarization. Non-USCIS documents are also often notarized and submitted in support of an immigration or naturalization petition. These might include translator's declarations, affidavits of relationship and statements from employers and banks.

If a USCIS-issued document does not have enough room for the Notary's seal, the Notary may affix his or her seal over boilerplate text (standard clauses or sections). Even though this procedure does not conform to generally recommended practice, federal officials advise that they prefer this over attaching a loose certificate.

Naturalization Certificates. It can be a serious violation of federal law to notarize or make a typewritten, photostatic or any other copy of a certificate of naturalization. Severe penalties, including imprisonment, are prescribed. The National Notary Association recommends against notarizing these documents unless specific instructions from a U.S. immigration official accompany the document and the form is to be submitted to the USCIS.

Translator's Declaration. A Notary may notarize the signature of a translator who certifies that a translation of a document the Notary does not understand is accurate and complete. The translator must sign an affidavit containing an oath or affirmation that the translation is accurate and complete and the affidavit must be attached to the document. In addition to the jurat wording, the notarial certificate for this affidavit must contain the title or type of document, the document date, the number of pages of the document and any additional signers other than those named in the notarial certificate (*ARS* 41-313[D] and 41-355[D]).

Incomplete Documents

Do Not Notarize. Arizona Notaries may not notarize any jurat on a document that contains blank spaces or is incomplete (*ARS* 41-328[A]). Although the statute does not specifically apply to acknowledgments, the Secretary of State and the National Notary Association recommend that a Notary never notarize a signature on any document with blank spaces (*ANPRM*).

Any blanks in a document should be filled in by the signer. If the blanks are inapplicable and intended to be left unfilled, the signer should be asked to line through each space (using ink) or to write "Not Applicable" or "N/A" (*ANPRM*).

Military-Officer Notarizations

May Notarize Worldwide. Active officers of the armed forces of the United States are federally commissioned to perform notarial functions for other members of the armed forces and their dependents anywhere in the world (*ARS* 26-160 and 33-501—33-508 and the Arizona Attorney General's Opinion I97-011). The following persons are authorized to act as Notaries (*ARS* 33-501):

- Judge advocates, including reserve judge advocates when not in a duty status

- Civilian attorneys serving as legal assistance attorneys

- Adjutants, assistant adjutants and personnel adjutants, including reserve members when not in a duty status

- Other members of the armed forces, including reserve members when not in a duty status, so authorized by armed-forces regulations or by statute

Validity of Notarial Acts. The signature of any of the above when acting as a Notary, together with his or her rank, or title and serial number is considered proof of the authority of that person to perform the act. Further proof of that officer's authority is not required. The signature and title of the person performing the act are *prima facie* evidence that he is a person with the designated title and that the signature is genuine (*ARS* 33-502).

Certificate. When taking an acknowledgement, military-officer Notaries make the same certifications that other Notaries in the state of Arizona make: that the person acknowledging appeared before the officer and acknowledged having signed the document, and that the person acknowledging was known to the person taking the acknowledgment or provided satisfactory evidence that he or she had the identity claimed (*ARS* 33-503). The certificate used by a military-officer Notary may either be a certificate prescribed for use in Arizona or one prescribed by the laws or regulations of the place in which the officer takes the acknowledgment, as long as it contains the words "acknowledged before me" or equivalent wording (*ARS* 33-504).

Authentication. Authentication of a military-officer notarization certificate is not required (*ARS* 41-322).

Fees. Military-officer Notaries may not charge or receive a fee for performing a notarial act (*ARS* 26-160).

Electronic Notarizations

Uniform Electronic Transactions Act. Effective July 18, 2000, the state adopted the Arizona Electronic Transactions Act (*ARS* 44-7001 through 44-7051). The *Arizona Administrative Code* (*AAC*) sets rules for electronic Notaries in Title 2 ("Administration"), Chapter 12 ("Office of the Secretary of State"), Article 12 ("Electronic Notary").

Notaries are permitted to perform notarial acts electronically where such acts are required by law without the imprint of the Notary's seal if the following conditions are met (*ARS* 44-7011):

1) The electronic document is signed pursuant to *ARS* 44-7001 through 44-7051 or section 41-132 in the presence of the Notary. (NOTE: Section 41-132 requires use of public key technology.)

2) The Notary confirms that the electronic signature on the electronic document is verifiably the signer's signature issued pursuant to *ARS* 44-7001 through 44-7051 or section 41-132.

3) The Notary signs the electronic document with an electronic signature that conforms to law.

4) The following information appears in electronic form within the document electronically signed by the Notary:

   (a) The Notary's full name and commission number exactly as it appears on the Notary's commission

   (b) The words "Electronic Notary Public," "State of Arizona" and "My commission expires on (date)"

   (c) The Notary's principal contact address exactly as it appears on the Notary's commission

   (d) The Notary's eMail or other electronic address exactly as it appears on the Notary's commission

Electronic Notary Commission. In Arizona, a separate commission is required in order to perform electronic notarizations. An Arizona Notary or any person meeting the qualifications may apply for an electronic Notary commission. In addition to the other qualifications that a person must fulfill in order to be an electronic Notary, as of July 29, 2010, he or she must also be a citizen or legal permanent resident of the United States (*ARS* 41-353[F]). An individual may simultaneously hold a "paper" and electronic Notary commission (*ARS* 41-353 and *AAC* R2-12-1201 and R2-12-1202).

To become an electronic Notary, the applicant must fill out a form provided by the Arizona Secretary of State and submit it to the Secretary (*AAC* R2-12-1201). Within 90 days of submitting the application, the applicant must register with the Secretary "possession of an approved electronic notary token" (*AAC* R2-12-1201). The application must include a $25,000 surety bond (*AAC* R2-12-1202).

Elements of a Notarized Electronic Document. A notarized electronic document has the following elements: a complete electronic document, the signer's signature or mark, the time stamp token and an electronic Notary token (*ARS* 41-355).

Time Token Required. For a Notary to notarize electronically, a signer must present a time stamp token that is created with approval of the Secretary of State and is in a form that reasonably verifies the signer's electronic signature and the time of the signing (*ARS* 44-7034). Any person or entity that can provide a service that synchronizes Mountain Standard Time into a process using an electronic Notary token or Notary service electronic certificate needs to meet the applicable technology standards required by *ARS* 41-132 (*AAC* R2-12-1206).

Electronic Notary Token. To obtain an electronic Notary token, evidence of an electronic Notary commission must first be presented to the provider. Only one token may be provided to a given electronic Notary (*AAC* R2-12-1204).

An electronic Notary token must contain the full name, commission number and commission expiration date of the electronic Notary, a link to the commission record of the electronic Notary on the Secretary of State's official website and any other applicable information relative to ARS 41-132 (*AAC* R2-12-1204).

Use of Electronic Tokens. Use of an electronic notary token is incomplete without incorporating the token elements into the document. The Notary may either directly incorporate the time and date of notarization or incorporate this time and date using a process of an approved time stamp provider. The Notary must also affix his or her electronic signature (*AAC* R2-12-1205).

Notarization in Electronic Notary's Presence. When a signer personally appears before the electronic Notary and makes a lawful and reasonable request for notarization, the electronic Notary may take electronic acknowledgments, administer oaths and affirmations or perform jurats relating to electronic documents and electronic notarial acts (*ARS* 41-355).

Electronic Notary Journal. The electronic Notary must "keep a journal of all electronic acts in bound paper form with the same form as required in *ARS* 41-319" (*AAC* R2-12-1203). If the electronic Notary also holds a regular Notary commission under *ARS* 41-312 and the commission dates are identical for the two commissions, then the electronic Notary may also use the regular journal as the required electronic Notary paper journal (*AAC* R2-12-1203). Otherwise, the electronic Notary must keep two journals.

"If a Notary Service Electronic Certificate is used in a manner to create an electronic signature in a notarial act, the document name, title, brief description of contents and the time stamp shall be entered into the issuing electronic notary's journal in a notary service electronic certificate entry" (*AAC* R2-12-1203).

For failure to deposit the electronic journal and records with the Secretary of State, a civil penalty of not more than $500 may be imposed (*AAC* R2-12-1209).

Fees for Electronic Notarial Acts. An electronic Notary may not charge more than $25 for any acknowledgment, oath or affirmation, jurat or other notarial act (*AAC* R2-12-1207).

Prohibited Acts and Penalties. An electronic Notary's commission may be suspended or revoked for many of the same offenses as a "paper" Notary. (See "Misconduct, Fines and Penalties," pages 71–79.) The penalties imposed for offenses by electronic Notaries are generally higher than those for ordinary Notaries (*ARS* 41-359, 360, 364, 367, 368 and *AAC* R2-12-1208).

Authentication

Documents Sent Out of State. Documents notarized in Arizona and sent to other states may be required to bear proof that the Notary's signature and seal are genuine and that the Notary had authority to act at the time of notarization. This process of proving the genuineness of an official signature and seal is called authentication or legalization. In Arizona, the proof is in the form of an authenticating certificate attached to the notarized document by the Secretary of State's office.

Documents notarized by an Arizona Notary and sent to foreign countries require either an *apostille* or a certificate of authentication issued by the Arizona Secretary of State's office. Depending on the destination country, this state certification is either an authentication or an *apostille*. In both cases, the certificate states that the notarial signature and seal on the document to which the certificate is attached belong to a Notary whose commission was valid at the time the notarization occurred.

Apostilles. More than 90 nations, including the United States, participate in a treaty that streamlines the authentication of notarized documents sent between any two of the participating nations. This treaty is called the *Hague Convention Abolishing the Requirement of Legalization for Foreign Public Documents*, hereafter simply called the Hague Convention. The Hague Convention permits one-step verification of a Notary's authority through the use of a standard certificate called an *apostille* (French for "notation"). When the Arizona Secretary of State or his or her agent issues an *apostille* for a notarized document bound for a country that participates in the Hague Convention, that certificate is the only proof of notarial authority required (See "Hague Convention Nations," pages 135–137. A list of these countries is available online at www.adoption.state.gov.) (*ARS* 41-326).

Authentications. For documents bound for a country that is not a participant in the Hague Convention, the Arizona Secretary of State or his or her agent issues a certificate of authentication (*ARS* 41-325). Certificates of authentication, unlike *apostilles*, vary in format from country to country and from jurisdiction to jurisdiction. Some countries accept a document bearing a single authentication certificate, while other countries require the document to be authenticated through a lengthier chain-certification process.

Chain Certifications. The chain-certification process can be quite complicated and time-consuming. It requires the attachment to the document of several different authenticating certificates. Each certificate in the chain-certification process validates the authenticity of the preceding certificate. Additional certificates of authority may need to be requested from the U.S. Department of State in Washington, D.C., a foreign consulate in Washington, D.C. and a ministry of foreign affairs in the particular foreign nation.

Requesting an *Apostille* or Authentication. Anyone who requests an *apostille* or a certificate of authentication should contact the Secretary of State's office. The Secretary of State's office is the only office in Arizona authorized to issue a certificate of authentication or *apostille* for a document going to a foreign country. The procedure for obtaining an *apostilles* and authenticating certificates is the same, except that an *apostille* must be specifically requested, and the country for which the document is destined should also be specified (*ARS* 41-325 and 41-326).

The fee for an *apostille* or an authenticating certificate is $3. The certificate may be obtained by mail or in person from:

> Arizona Secretary of State
> Attention: Notary Section
> 1700 W. Washington Street, 7th Floor
> Phoenix, AZ 85007-2888
> (602) 542-4758

MISCONDUCT, FINES AND PENALTIES

Official Misconduct

Definition. Official misconduct is defined as a Notary's performance of a prohibited act, failure to perform any required act or performance of an official act in a manner found to be grossly negligent or against the public interest. Official misconduct by a Notary is grounds for the Secretary of State to refuse to appoint a person as a Notary or to suspend or revoke a Notary's commission. Acts of misconduct may be infractions, misdemeanors or felonies.

Infractions. Infractions are minor violations of the law that are considered less serious than other crimes. Typically, a Notary is guilty of an infraction when he or she violates a rule, law or regulation. Infractions generally do not result in the loss of liberty or imprisonment. They may, however, be punishable by fines and the loss of certain privileges.

Misdemeanors. Most acts of criminal misconduct by Notaries are classified as misdemeanors, which are less harmful crimes than felonies and are punishable by fines of less than $1,000 and/or jail terms of less than one year.

Felonies. Considered to be more harmful crimes, felonies are in most cases punished with larger fines and longer imprisonment than misdemeanors, with prison terms served in a penitentiary rather than a jail.

Penalties for Misconduct

Liability. Notaries have unlimited personal liability for financial damages resulting from their misconduct or negligence, whether intentional or unintentional. The fact that a mistake was not deliberate cannot prevent a lawsuit or protect a Notary from financial liability. For a given act of misconduct, a Notary may suffer administrative, criminal, and civil penalties. In Arizona, the employer of the Notary could also be liable if it is determined that the employer had actual knowledge of, or reasonably should have known of, the misconduct (*ANPRM*).

Administrative Penalties. Administrative penalties include but are not limited to suspending a Notary's commission and removing a Notary from office. The Secretary of State may suspend a Notary's commission for between 30 and 180 days (*ARS* 41-330[C] and 41-368[C]).

The Secretary of State may also remove a Notary from office by revoking his or her commission. When a Notary's commission is revoked, the individual is stripped of all notarial powers and may not serve the rest of his or her term. As of July 29, 2010, if the Secretary of State revokes a Notary's commission, the Secretary may refuse to reappoint that person as a Notary Public for an indefinite period of time (*ARS* 41-330). A Notary whose commission has been revoked must send his or her seal, journal, commission certificate and any other records to the Secretary of State's office (*ARS* 41-317[A]).

New legislation effective in 2010 and 2011 authorizes the Secretary of State to require suspended Notaries to present proof of attendance at a Notary training course before reinstatement of a suspended commission. The Secretary may assess a fee for administering training courses and any fee collected must be deposited collected in the Notary education fund established by section 41-332 (*ARS* 41-312[F] and 41-353[I]).

Before a commission is suspended or revoked, however, the Notary is entitled to a hearing. The Secretary of State must notify the Notary of such a hearing and give the Notary the chance to participate (*ARS* 41-330[E] and 41-368[E]).

Criminal Penalties. A crime is a serious violation of law for which the penalty is a fine, imprisonment or both. Notaries most often are criminally prosecuted when their misconduct is part of a more comprehensive violation.

Civil Penalties. Misconduct or negligence also exposes the Notary to civil lawsuits to recover financial losses. Civil suits may result in court verdicts or out-of-court settlements that require the Notary to pay for damages. They also involve attorney fees and other legal defense costs for which the Notary is responsible. A Notary and the surety company bonding the Notary may be sued by any person, corporation or other entity seeking compensation for financial damages caused by a Notary's alleged misconduct. The surety is liable only up to the $5,000 amount of the bond, but a Notary may be found liable for any amount of money.

Prohibited Acts

Misstatement or Omission on Application. Substantial and material misstatement or omission in the application for a Notary commission is grounds for the Secretary of State to deny, suspend or revoke a commission (*ARS* 41-330[A][1] and 41-368[A][1]). If the Secretary of State denies a commission, the Secretary must notify the applicant within 30 days and state the reasons for the denial (*ARS* 41-330[B] and 41-368[B]).

Insufficient Funds for Fees. A Notary's commission may be denied, suspended or revoked if a check for application fees or bond fees is returned (*ARS* 41-330[A][11] and 41-368[A][12]).

Failure to Provide Copy of Commission Certificate. Any Notary who fails to provide a photocopy of the Notary commission for any seal vendor who manufactures a Notary seal is guilty of a Class 3 Misdemeanor. Similarly, any seal vendor who fails to retain a photocopy of the Notary's commission certificate for four years is guilty of a Class 3 Misdemeanor (*ARS* 41-321).

Dishonest, Fraudulent or Deceptive Conduct. Engaging in any fraudulent or deceptive conduct that is related in any way to one's capacity as a Notary Public with the intent to substantially benefit the Notary or another person or to substantially injure another person is considered official misconduct. The Secretary of State may revoke, suspend or deny a Notary's commission (*ARS* 41-330[A][7] and 41-368[A][7]).

Failure of Duty. A Notary who fails to faithfully and fully discharge the duties and responsibilities of a Notary may have his or her commission denied, suspended or revoked by the Secretary of State (*ARS* 41-330[A][4] and 41-368[A][4]).

Failure of duty includes, but is not limited to, the following:

- Notarizing without using a Notary seal

- Notarizing without using notarial certificate language

- Notarizing a document containing blank spaces

Failure to Cooperate with an Investigation. A Notary's failure to respond to a Notary complaint by the Secretary of State or Attorney General may lead to the Notary's commission being denied, suspended or revoked (*ARS* 41-313[B][4], 41-331[B] and 41-370[B]).

Conviction of Felony. Conviction for a felony or any offense involving moral turpitude or that has a reasonable relationship to the functions of the office of Notary Public is reason for the Secretary of State to deny, suspend or revoke a commission even if the Notary's civil rights have been restored (*ARS* 41-330[A][2] and 41-368 [A][2]).

If a Notary is convicted of a felony before the end of his or her term of commission, the Secretary of State may revoke the Notary's commission (Arizona Attorney General Opinion I79-305, December 30, 1979). Once a Notary has been convicted of a felony, the Notary may no longer perform notarial duties. The Notary must turn in his or her seal, journal, commission certificate and any other records to the Secretary of State's office (*ARS* 41-317[A]).

Revocation of Professional License. Any revocation, suspension, restriction or denial of a professional license if that action was for misconduct, dishonesty or any cause that relates to a Notary's duties is grounds for the Secretary of State to revoke or suspend a commission (*ARS* 41-330[A][3] and 41-368[A][3]).

Failure to Notify of Name or Address Change. Any person who fails to notify the Secretary of State within 30 days of a change to his or her surname, or a mailing, business or residential address change is subject to a $25 civil penalty. A signed notice of the change, including both the new and old surname or the new and old address must be delivered by certified mail or other means that provide a receipt. There is no penalty for failing to notify the Secretary of State about a change of business address (*ARS* 41-323, 41-327 and 41-364).

Failure to Notify of Lost or Stolen Seal or Journal. Any person who fails to notify the Secretary of State of a lost or stolen seal is subject to a $25 civil penalty and faces possible commission denial, suspension or revocation for failure of duty. This signed notification must be delivered or mailed within 10 days after the loss or theft to the Secretary of State's office by certified mail or other means that would provide a receipt. In the case of theft, the Notary also must inform the local law enforcement agency (*ARS* 41-323 and 41-364).

Using False or Misleading Advertising. The use of false or misleading advertising by a Notary to represent that he or she has duties, qualifications, powers, rights and privileges not given by law is cause for the Secretary of State to deny, revoke or suspend a Notary commission (*ARS* 41-329, 41-330[A][5] and 41-368[A][5]).

Overcharging. Charging more than the legally prescribed fees is a Class 5 Felony. In addition, if a Notary charges a higher fee than what is prescribed by statute, then the Notary will be liable to the overcharged party for four times the amount unlawfully demanded and received (*ARS* 38-413 and 41-316[C]). And, the Secretary of State may deny, suspend or revoke the Notary's commission (*ARS* 41-330[A][6] and 41-368[A][6]).

Advertising or Charging Unauthorized Fee. A Notary may not advertise or charge a fee for a notarial act that is not specifically authorized by the Secretary of State in administrative rule (*ARS* 41-316[C] and 41-358[C], and *AAC* R2-12-1102 and R2-12-1207).

Notarization without Signer Present. A Notary may not notarize the signature of someone who is not present (*ARS* 41-313[B][1] and 41-355[B][1]).

Failure to Positively Identify Signer. Failing to take all reasonable steps to verify a signer's identity could subject the Notary to criminal fraud, civil liability and the denial or revocation of the commission by the Secretary of State (*ANPRM*).

Notarization of Own Signature. A Notary may not notarize his or her own signature (*ARS* 41-328[B] and 41-366[B]).

Notarization with Direct Material Benefit. A Notary may not notarize a document in which the Notary has a direct material benefit (*ARS* 41-328[C] and 41-366[C]).

Notarization with Other Conflict of Interest. A Notary may not perform a notarization on a document if the Notary is a party to the document or an officer of any named party (*ARS* 41-41-328[C] and 366[C]).

Notarization for Certain Relatives. A Notary may not notarize the signature of any person who is related to the Notary by marriage or adoption (*ARS* 41-328[B] and 41-366[B]).

Notarization of False Documents. Any person who knowingly notarizes a document that he or she knows to be false or forged is guilty of a Class 6 Felony. The same punishment applies to anyone who offers to file, register or record in an Arizona public office a document known to be false or forged (*ARS* 39-161).

Notarization of Incomplete Documents. A jurat may not be performed when a document contains blank spaces or is otherwise incomplete, and the Secretary of State recommends that a Notary refuse to notarize a signature on any document that contains blank spaces (*ARS* 41-328[A], 41-366[B] and *ANPRM*).

Certification of False Statements. A Notary who signs a certificate or certifies a writing containing a statement which he or she knows to be false is guilty of a Class 6 Felony and may have the commission denied, suspended or revoked by the Secretary of State (*ARS* 38-423 and 41-330[A][10] and 41-368[A][10]).

NOTARY LAWS EXPLAINED

Failure to Complete Certificate. The Secretary of State may deny, suspend or revoke a Notary commission if a Notary fails to complete the acknowledgment or jurat wording at the time of notarization (*ARS* 41-330[A][8] and 41-368[A][8]).

Notarization without Certificate. The Secretary of State may deny, suspend or revoke a Notary commission of the Notary notarizes a document without completing a notarial certificate. In addition, such incomplete notarizations may be declared invalid in a court of law. Simply "stamping and signing" a document without notarial wording is prohibited (*ARS* 41-330[A][12] and 41-368[A][12]).

Notarization without Seal. Arizona law requires that the Notary's official seal be placed on each notarized document. Without the official seal, the notarization is incomplete, and may be declared invalid in a court of law (*ANPRM*).

Failure to Administer Oath/Affirmation. For failing to administer an oath or affirmation as part of a jurat, the Notary's commission might be denied, suspended or revoked (*ARS* 41-330[A][9] and 41-368[A][9]). A Notary must not perform a jurat notarization when a signer has not personally signed in the presence of the Notary (*ANPRM*).

Use of Seal by Another. A Seal may be used only by the commissioned Notary whose information appears on the seal. A Notary may not use another Notary's seal or knowingly let someone else use his or her seal (*ANPRM*).

Notarization of Naturalization Certificate Copies. A Notary may be in violation of federal law if he or she notarizes or makes a typewritten, photostatic or any other copy of a certificate of naturalization.

Destruction of Notary Records. Any person who knowingly destroys, defaces or conceals a Notary's journal, journal entry or any other records belonging to the office of a Notary Public may be fined up to $500 and is liable for damages to any party injured (*ARS* 41-318 and 41-360).

Failure to Surrender Notarial Records. If a Notary fails to turn in his or her records within three months after ending his or her notarial career, that Notary will be fined $50 to $500.If the

Notary dies, the Notary's personal representative must surrender the Notary's records within three months of appointment as the Notary's representative. Otherwise, the representative may be fined $50 to $500 (*ARS* 41-317 and 41-359).

Errors and Omissions Insurance

Purpose. Errors and omissions (E&O) insurance covers the insured Notary, up to the policy's limit, for legal costs resulting from any unintentional error made by the Notary during the term of the policy, provided that the error was directly related to the insured's notarial duties. E&O policies usually do not cover non-notarial acts or notarial acts that are dishonest, fraudulent, illegal, criminal, malicious, libelous or slanderous.

Liability. E&O insurance will pay out damages to an injured party after a court verdict or out-of-court settlement. The Notary does not need to reimburse the insurance company for any payments made on his or her behalf.

Most E&O policies also include arranging for the Notary's defense and absorbing the Notary's attorney fees and other defense costs. The Notary need not go to the trouble of finding an attorney, since the insurance company's attorneys will handle the defense. These attorneys often are able to have lawsuits dismissed or to negotiate out-of-court settlements.

Purchase. Purchasing this type of insurance is not required by law. However, the Secretary of State and the NNA recommend that each Notary purchase a policy. E&O insurance may be purchased or cancelled by the Notary at any time.

Reasonable Care

High Standard of Conduct. As a public official, a Notary is held to a high standard of conduct. Whenever a Notary performs a notarial act, he or she is expected to exercise what is known as "reasonable care." Reasonable care is the level of attentiveness and concern expected of a person of ordinary intelligence. The first rule of reasonable care is strict adherence to all laws governing Notaries and notarization. In situations not explicitly covered by statute, a Notary should make every effort to use common sense and behave in a responsible and ethical fashion, following the accepted standards of conduct and best practices for that situation.

A Notary is someone others depend upon for impartiality and honesty. In order for notarial acts to be respected as they should be, Notaries must maintain the public trust and confidence. The Notary therefore should not be involved with any document or transaction that is false, deceptive or fraudulent or which will violate the legal rights or interests of members of the public. He or she may be subject to certain penalties (such as commission revocation), even when an infraction has nothing to do with a notarization but nonetheless casts doubt on the Notary's integrity.

Fraud Deterrent. Deterring fraud is the Notary's most important role. Fraud may be defined as any deception aimed at causing a person to unknowingly surrender money, property, rights or advantages without appropriate compensation for the item(s) surrendered. A Notary should exercise reasonable care not only because failure to do so may result in disciplinary measures or a lawsuit to recover financial damages caused by an error, but also because the Notary's actions may facilitate a fraud that harms the very members of the public whom the Notary has been commissioned to protect. If, on the other hand, a Notary can convincingly show that he or she used reasonable care when performing a notarization, the public will be protected and the Notary will be shielded from liability in the event that the notarization is challenged. ■

Test Your Knowledge

Trial Exam

Purpose. This examination is designed to test your knowledge of the basic concepts of notarization.

Structure. A perfect score is 100 points. The exam is structured as follows:

- Twenty true/false questions worth 1 point each.
- Five multiple-choice questions worth 4 points each.
- Five fill-in-the-blank questions worth 4 points each.
- Five essay questions worth 8 points each.

Instructions. To complete the exam, you will need a pen or pencil and a separate sheet of paper for your answers to the essay questions. Work through the exam without looking at the answers, then check your responses and note where you need additional study. You will find the correct answers to all exam questions on pages 83–85.

Part 1: True/False. For the following statements, answer true or false. Each correct answer is worth 1 point:

1. Notaries may act only in the county where they are commissioned. True or false?

2. The maximum Notary fee for taking the acknowledgment of three signers is $15. True or false?

3. It is a Notary's duty to serve all persons requesting lawful notarial acts, even those who are not customers. True or false?

TEST YOUR KNOWLEDGE

4. Notaries must keep a photocopy of every document notarized. True or false?

5. An Arizona Notary may take a deposition, oral testimony that is written down and used as evidence in a court proceeding. True or false?

6. Notaries may withhold their services if they believe a signer is being coerced into signing a document. True or false?

7. It is a Notary's duty to draft powers of attorney, mortgages and deeds upon request. True or false?

8. The letters "L.S." stand for the Latin words *locus sigilli,* which mean "location of the seal." True or false?

9. Holographic wills must be notarized in order to be valid. True or false?

10. A Notary may rely on a stranger as a credible person as long as the individual has an acceptable photo ID. True or false?

11. A Notary may notarize signatures on documents which he or she will be signing as a corporate officer. True or false?

12. A signer of a homestead agreement for property in Arizona must leave a right thumbprint in the Notary's journal. True or false?

13. The Notary need not reimburse the surety company for bond funds paid out to a person financially harmed by the Notary's actions. True or false?

14. When a person signs a document as a corporate officer, a Notary must verify that he or she has the authority to sign the document in the stated capacity. True or false?

15. A Notary's public-records journal belongs to the Notary's employer if the employer paid for it. True or false?

16. An acknowledgment certificate may not be used for jurats. True or false?

ARIZONA NOTARY LAW PRIMER

17. An affirmation is the legal equivalent of an oath, but has no reference to a Supreme Being. True or false?

18. A county recorder will not accept a notarial certificate printed in 9-point type. True or false?

19. Notaries may not refuse to notarize a jurat on a blank or incomplete document as long as it is signed in the Notary's presence. True or false?

20. A Notary may certify a copy of a college diploma. True or false?

Multiple Choice. Choose the one best answer to each question. Each correct answer is worth 4 points.

1. A Notary has a disqualifying interest when notarizing which of the following?
   a. An employer's signature
   b. A grandchild's signature
   c. His or her own signature

2. Which of the following must be true in order for an applicant to become a Notary?
   a. The applicant has been a state resident for at least one year
   b. The applicant is at least 18 years old
   c. The applicant has passed an oral exam given by the Secretary of State's office

3. A certificate of authority validating a Notary's commission may be obtained from which of the following?
   a. The Governor's office or the county clerk
   b. The Notary himself/herself
   c. The Secretary of State

4. An acceptable ID may be which of the following?
   a. An unexpired Mexican driver license
   b. An unexpired foreign passport
   c. An unexpired U.S. Armed Forces identification card

TEST YOUR KNOWLEDGE

5. An Arizona Notary is permitted to do which of the following?
   a. Notarize a signature made by mark
   b. Certify copies of computer software
   c. Certify a copy of a foreign birth certificate

Fill in the Blank. Write in the word or phrase that best completes each sentence. Each correct answer is worth 4 points.

1. The Notary and the Notary's _____ are liable for the Notary's neglect or official misconduct.

2. A solemn, spoken pledge that is not an affirmation is called an _____.

3. An acceptable ID card must contain a signature, a physical description and a _____ of its bearer.

4. A certified copy certifies the _____ of the reproduction.

5. Wills written entirely in the testator's own handwriting are called _____.

Essay. Reply to each question or statement with a short paragraph. Each complete and correct response is worth 8 points.

1. Discuss the distinctions between a Notary bond and Notary errors and omissions insurance.

2. Outline the components of satisfactory evidence of identity and what documents can be used to meet the requirements.

3. What is an *apostille* and when is it used?

4. Why should a Notary always complete the journal entry before filling out a notarial certificate?

5. Outline the differences between what a Notary certifies on an acknowledgment certificate and a jurat certificate.

Test Answers
True/False. 1. F; 2. F; 3 T; 4. F; 5 F; 6. T; 7. F; 8. T; 9. F; 10. T;

ARIZONA NOTARY LAW PRIMER

11. F; 12. F; 13. F; 14. T; 15. F; 16. T; 17. T; 18. T; 19. F; 20. T

Multiple Choice. 1. c; 2. b; 3. c; 4. c; 5. a

Fill In The Blank. 1. Surety; 2. Oath; 3. Photograph; 4. Accuracy; 5. Holographic

Essay. Responses should include the basic information in the paragraphs below:

1. A Notary bond, obtained through a state-licensed surety company, provides protection for the public in case of the Notary's negligence or intentional misconduct. Up to the face amount of the bond, the surety agrees to pay damages to anyone who suffers a loss because of the Notary's actions; the Notary, however, then must reimburse the surety. Notary errors and omissions insurance, also purchased from a state-licensed company, protects the Notary in case of the Notary's unintentional error, up to the policy limit. The Notary does not reimburse the insurance company. A bond is required by law; errors and omissions insurance is not.

2. Identity may be satisfactorily proven in one of three ways:
   1) the Notary's personal knowledge of a signer
   2) an ID card that is a current driver's license issued by a U.S. state or territory, a current U.S. passport, a current military ID card, or any other current ID card issued by the U.S. government or any state or tribal government that contains the individual's photograph, signature and physical description consisting of the individual's height, weight, color of hair and color of eyes
   3) the oath or affirmation of a credible person who personally knows the Notary and the signer or the oath or affirmation of a credible person who personally knows the signer and presents an acceptable ID card to the Notary

3. An *apostille* is a certificate that verifies or authenticates the signature and seal of a Notary. It is issued under the provisions of an international treaty, signed by more than 90 nations, called the *Hague Convention Abolishing the Requirement of Legalization for Foreign Public Documents*. For notarized documents exchanged

between the subscribing nations, this treaty streamlines the time-consuming authentication process known as "chain certification" by requiring only one authenticating certificate, the *apostille* (French for "notation"). *Apostilles* for Arizona Notaries are issued by the Secretary of State.

4. Filling out a journal entry before completing a notarial certificate prevents a signer from leaving with the document before an important record of the notarization is made in the journal.

5. On an acknowledgment certificate, a Notary certifies that the signer of the document personally appeared before the Notary on the date and in the county indicated, that the signer's identity was satisfactorily proven to the Notary and that the signer acknowledged having voluntarily signed the document. On a jurat certificate, a Notary certifies that the signer of the document personally appeared before the Notary on the date and in the county indicated, that the signer's identity was satisfactorily proven to the Notary, that the signer signed the document in the Notary's presence and that the Notary administered an oath or affirmation to the signer.

Tally Your Score

After checking your answers, add up your score. Then look at the grading scale below to determine how you stand:

- 90–100:   Excellent!
- 80–89:   Good, but you need some review.
- 70–79:   Fair. Reread the parts of the *Prime*r covering the answers you missed.
- Below 70: Below par. Study the laws thoroughly again. ■

Arizona Laws Pertaining to Notaries Public

Any statutes or administrative codes cited in this *Primer* but not reproduced in this section may be found on the state's websites:

- *Arizona Revised Statutes*: http://www.azleg.state.az.us/ArizonaRevisedStatutes.asp

- *Arizona Administrative Code*: http://www.azsos.gov/public_Services/Title_09/9-10.htm

---

ARIZONA REVISED STATUTES
Title 41. State Government
Chapter 2. Administrative Officers
Article 2. Notaries Public

§ 41-311. Definitions

In this article, unless the context otherwise requires:

1. "Acknowledgment" means a notarial act in which a notary certifies that a signer, whose identity is proven by satisfactory evidence, appeared before the notary and acknowledged that the signer signed the document.

2. "Commission" means to authorize to perform notarial acts and the written authority to perform those acts.

3. "Copy certification" means a notarial act in which the notary certifies that the notary has made a photocopy of an original document that is neither a public record nor publicly recordable.

4. "Incomplete document" means a document that has not been signed where a signature line is provided or where other obvious blanks appear in the document or that lacks a notarial certificate.

5. "Jurat" means a notarial act in which the notary certifies that a signer, whose identity is proven by satisfactory evidence, has made in the notary's presence a voluntary signature and has taken an oath or affirmation

vouching for the truthfulness of the signed document.
6. "Notarial act" or "notarization" means any act that a notary is authorized to perform under section 41 313.
7. "Notarial certificate" or "certificate" means the part of or attachment to a notarized document for completion by the notary that bears the notary's signature and seal and states the venue, date and facts that are attested by the notary in a particular notarization.
8. "Notary public" or "notary" means any person commissioned to perform notarial acts under this article.
9. "Oath" or "affirmation" means a notarial act or part of a notarial act in which a person made a vow in the presence of the notary under penalty of perjury, with reference made to a supreme being in the case of an oath.
10. "Personal knowledge" means familiarity with an individual resulting from interactions with that individual over a sufficient time to eliminate reasonable doubt that the individual has the identity claimed.
11. "Satisfactory evidence of identity" means:
(a) Proof of identity is evidenced by one of the following:
(i) An unexpired driver license that is issued by a state or territory of the United States.
(ii) An unexpired passport that is issued by the United States department of state.
(iii) An unexpired identification card that is issued by any branch of the United States armed forces.
(iv) Any other unexpired identification card that is issued by the united states government or a state or tribal government, that contains the individual's photograph, signature and physical description and that contains the individual's height, weight, color of hair and color of eyes.
(v) The oath or affirmation of a credible person who is personally known to the notary and who personally knows the individual.
(vi) The oath or affirmation of a credible person who personally knows the individual and who provides satisfactory evidence of identity pursuant to item (i), (ii), (iii) or (iv) of this subdivision.
(vii) Personal knowledge of the individual by the notary.
(b) In addition to subdivision (a), for the purposes of a real estate conveyance or financing proof of identity may be evidenced by one of the following:
(i) A valid unexpired passport that is issued by the United States government.
(ii) A valid unexpired passport that is issued by a national government other than the United States government and that is accompanied by a valid unexpired visa or other documentation that is issued by the United States government and that is necessary to establish an individual's legal presence in the United States.
(iii) Any other valid unexpired identification that is deemed acceptable by the United States Department of Homeland Security to establish an individual's legal presence in the United States and that is accompanied with supporting documents as required by the United States Department of Homeland Security.
12. "Venue" means this state and county where a notarial act occurs.

ARIZONA NOTARY LAW PRIMER

§ 41-312. Appointment; term; oath and bond

A. The secretary of state may appoint notaries public in each county to hold office for four years who shall have jurisdiction in the county in which they reside and in which they are appointed. Acknowledgments of documents may be taken and executed and oaths may be administered by a notary public in any county of the state although the commission is issued to the notary public in and for another county.

B. The secretary of state shall give notice of the appointment to the person appointed who shall take, within twenty days after receiving such notice, the oath prescribed by law and give a bond, with sureties approved by the state, in an amount prescribed by the secretary of state and file it with the secretary of state. On filing the official oath and bond, the secretary of state shall deliver the commission to such person.

C. A notary public is a public officer commissioned by this state and the following apply without regard to whether the notary public's employer or any other person has paid the fees and costs for the commissioning of the notary public, including costs for the official seal and journals:

1. A notary public's official seal and commission and any journal that contains only public record entries remain the property of the notary public.

2. A notary public may perform notarizations outside the workplace of the notary's employer except during those times normally designated as the notary public's hours of duty for that employer. All fees received by a notary public for notarial services provided while not on duty remain the property of the notary public.

3. An employer of a notary public shall not limit the notary public's services to customers or other persons designated by the employer.

D. A notary public shall continue to serve until the notary public's commission expires, the notary public resigns the commission, the notary public dies or the secretary of state revokes the commission. An employer may not cancel the notary bond or notary commission of any notary public who is an employee and who leaves that employment.

E. A notary public shall comply with all of the following:
1. Be at least eighteen years of age.
2. Be a citizen or a legal permanent resident of the United States.
3. Be a resident of this state for income tax purposes and claim the individual's residence in this state as the individual's primary residence on state and federal tax returns.
4. Except as provided in section 41 330, subsection A, paragraph 2, never have been convicted of a felony.
5. Keep as a reference a manual that is approved by the secretary of state and that describes the duties, authority and ethical responsibilities of notaries public.
6. Be able to read and write English.

F. An applicant for appointment and commission as a notary public shall complete an application form prescribed by the secretary of state. Except for the applicant's name and business address, all information on the application is confidential and may not be disclosed to any person other than the applicant, the applicant's personal representative or an employee or officer of the federal, state or local government who is acting in an official capacity. The secretary of state shall use the information contained on the application only for carrying out the purposes of this article.

G. This state or any of its political subdivisions may pay the fees and costs for the commissioning of a notary public who is an employee of this state or any of its political subdivisions and who performs notarial services in the course of the notary public's employment or for the convenience of public employees.

H. The secretary of state may require that applicants and suspended Notaries present proof of attendance at a notary training course before receiving their commissions or before reinstatement of a suspended commission. Any applicant who is required to attend a notary training course must complete the training within ninety days before renewing their commissions. The secretary of state may assess a fee prescribed by the secretary of state for administering notary training courses. The secretary of state shall deposit the fees collected in the notary education fund established by section 41 332.

§ 41-313. Duties

A. Notaries public shall perform the following notarial acts, when requested:
1. Take acknowledgments and give certificates of the acknowledgments endorsed on or attached to the instrument.
2. Administer oaths and affirmations.
3. Perform jurats.
4. Perform copy certification.

B. Notaries public shall perform the notarial acts prescribed in Subsection A of this section only if:
1. The signer is in the presence of the notary at the time of notarization.
2. The signer signs in a language that the notary understands.
3. Subject to Subsection D, the signer communicates directly with the notary in a language they both understand or indirectly through a translator who is physically present with the signer and notary at the time of the notarization and communicates directly with the signer and the notary in languages the translator understands.
4. The notarial certificate is worded and completed using only letters, characters and a language that are read, written and understood by the notary public.

C. If a notary attaches a notarial certificate to a document using a separate sheet of paper, the attachment must contain a description of the document that includes at a minimum the title or type of document, the document date, the number of pages of the document and any additional signers other than those named in the notarial certificate.

D. A notary may perform a notarial act on a document that is a translation of a document that is in a language that the notary does not understand only if the person performing the translation signs an affidavit containing an oath or affirmation that the translation is accurate and complete. The notarized translation and affidavit shall be attached to the document and shall contain all of the elements described in Subsection C.

ARIZONA NOTARY LAW PRIMER

E. Notaries public shall:
1. Keep, maintain and protect as a public record a journal of all official acts performed by the notary as described in section 41 319.
2. Provide and keep the official seal that is imprinted in dark ink with the words "notary public", the name of the county in which the notary is commissioned, the name of the notary as it appears on the notarial application, the great seal of the state of Arizona and the expiration date of the notarial commission.
3. Authenticate with the official seal all official acts on every certificate or acknowledgment signed and sealed by the notary.
4. Respond to any requests for information and comply with any investigations that are initiated by the secretary of state or the attorney general.

§ 41-314. Notary bond fund; purpose; exemption
A. The notary bond fund is established consisting of monies received pursuant to section 41-178.

B. The secretary of state shall administer the fund and spend monies in the fund in order to defray the cost of the secretary of state's office assuming the responsibilities associated with the processing and administration of notary bonds.

C. On notice from the secretary of state, the state treasurer shall invest and divest monies in the fund as provided by section 35-313, and monies earned from investment shall be credited to the fund.

D. Monies in the fund are continuously appropriated and exempt from the provisions of section 35-190 relating to lapsing of appropriations.

§ 41-315. Bond
A. A person who has been commissioned as a notary shall file with the secretary of state an oath of office and a bond in an amount prescribed by the secretary of state in order for the commission to become effective. A licensed surety shall execute the bond. The bond shall be effective for four years beginning on the commission's effective date.

B. The secretary of state shall not accept any bond that was issued more than sixty days before or more than thirty days after the date on which the secretary of state commissions a notary.

§ 41-316. Fees
A. The secretary of state shall establish fees that notaries public may charge for notarial acts. These fees shall be established by rules adopted pursuant to chapter 6 of this title.

B. Notaries public may be paid an amount up to the amount authorized for mileage expenses and per diem subsistence for state employees as prescribed by title 38, chapter 4, article 2.

C. A notary shall not advertise or charge or receive a fee for performing a notarial act except as specifically authorized by rule.

§ 41-317. Delivering notary seal, notarial journal and records; failure to comply; storing records; certified copies
A. On the resignation or revocation of a notarial commission or the death

of a notary, the notary seal, notarial journal and records, except those records of notarial acts that are not public record, shall be delivered by certified mail or other means providing a receipt to the secretary of state. If a notary does not apply for reappointment, on expiration of the notarial commission the notary seal, journal and records shall be delivered to the secretary of state as required for resignation under this subsection. A notary who neglects for three months thereafter to deposit such records, seal and papers, or the personal representative of a deceased notary who neglects for three months after his appointment to deposit such records, seal and papers, shall forfeit to the state not less than fifty nor more than five hundred dollars.

B. While a notary public is commissioned, a notary public shall keep all records and journals of the notary's acts for at least five years after the date the notarial act was performed. On receipt of the records and journals from a notary public who no longer is commissioned, the secretary of state shall keep all records and journals of notaries public deposited in the secretary of state's office for five years and shall give certified copies thereof when required, and for the copy certifications the secretary of state shall receive the same fees as are by law allowed to notaries public. The copy certifications shall be as valid and effectual as if given by a notary public.

§ 41-318. Willful destruction of records; penalty

Any person who knowingly destroys, defaces or conceals any journal entry or records belonging to the office of a notary public shall forfeit to the state an amount not exceeding five hundred dollars and shall be liable for damages to any party injured thereby.

§ 41-319. Journal

A. The notary shall keep a paper journal and, except as prescribed by subsection E, shall keep only one journal at a time. The notary shall record all notarial acts in chronological order. The notary shall furnish, when requested, a certified copy of any public record in the notary's journal. Records of notarial acts that violate the attorney client privilege or that are confidential pursuant to federal or state law are not a public record. Each journal entry shall include at least:

1. The date of the notarial act.
2. A description of the document or type of notarial act.
3. The printed full name, signature and address of each person for whom a notarial act is performed.
4. The type of satisfactory evidence of identity presented to the notary by each person for whom a notarial act is performed, if other than the notary's personal knowledge of the individual is used as satisfactory evidence of identity.
5. A description of the identification document, its serial or identification number and its date of issuance or expiration.
6. The fee, if any, charged for the notarial act.

B. If a notary has personal knowledge of the identity of a signer, the requirements of subsection A, paragraphs 1 through 5 may be satisfied by the notary retaining a paper or electronic copy of the notarized documents for each notarial act.

C. If a notary does more than one notarization for an individual within a six month period, the notary shall have the individual provide satisfactory evidence of identity the first time the notary performs the notarization for the individual but may not require satisfactory evidence of identity or the individual to sign the journal for subsequent notarizations performed for the individual during the six month period.

D. If a notary performs more than one notarization of the same type for a signer either on like documents or within the same document and at the same time, the notary may group the documents together and make one journal entry for the transaction.

E. If one or more entries in a notary public's journal are not public records, the notary public may keep one journal that contains entries that are not public records and one journal that contains entries that are public records. A notary public's journal that contains entries that are not public records is the property of the employer of that notary public and shall be retained by that employer if the notary public leaves that employment. A notary public's journal that contains only public records is the property of the notary public without regard to whether the notary public's employer purchased the journal or provided the fees for the commissioning of the notary public.

F. Except as provided in subsections A and E, the notary's journal is a public record that may be viewed by or copied for any member of the public, but only upon presentation to the notary of a written request that details the month and year of the notarial act, the name of the person whose signature was notarized and the type of document or transaction.

§ 41-320. Competency of bank and corporation notaries

A. It is lawful for a notary public who is a stockholder, director, officer or employee of a corporation to take the acknowledgment or oath of any party to any written instrument executed to or by the corporation, or to administer an oath to any other stockholder, director, officer, employee or agent of the corporation, or to protest for nonacceptance or nonpayment of bills of exchange, drafts, checks, notes and other negotiable instruments which may be owned or held for collection by the corporation.

B. It is unlawful for any notary public to take the acknowledgment of an instrument executed by or to a corporation of which he is a stockholder, director, officer or employee, where the notary is a party to the instrument, either individually or as a representative of the corporation, or to protest any negotiable instrument owned or held for collection by the corporation, where the notary is individually a party to the instrument.

§ 41-321. Obtaining a seal; violation; classification

A. A vendor of notary seals may not provide an official seal to a person unless the person presents a photocopy of the person's notarial commission. The vendor shall retain the photocopy for four years.

B. A notary public's official seal may be any shape and shall produce a stamped seal that is no more than one and one half inches high and two and one half inches wide. A notary public may possess only one official seal but may also possess and use an embossing seal that may be used only in conjunction with the notary public's official seal. An embossing seal is not an official seal of a notary public.

C. A person who violates this section is guilty of a class 3 misdemeanor.

§ 41-322. Authentication of authority of officer for foreign notarizations

A. If a notarial act is performed by any of the persons described in section 33 501, paragraphs 1 through 4, other than a person authorized to perform notarial acts by the laws or regulations of a foreign country, the signature, rank or title and serial number, if any, of the person is sufficient proof of the authority of the person to perform the act. Further proof of the person's authority is not required.

B. If a notarial act is performed by a person authorized by the laws or regulations of a foreign country to perform the act, any of the following is sufficient proof of the authority of the person to perform the act:

1. Certification by a foreign service officer of the United States resident in the country in which the notarial act is performed or a diplomatic or consular officer of the foreign country resident in the United States that a person who holds the office that the person holds is authorized to perform notarial acts.

2. Affixation to the notarized document of the official seal of the person performing the notarial act.

3. The appearance either in a digest of foreign law or in a list that is customarily used as a source of such information of the title and the indication of authority to perform notarial acts of the person.

C. If a notarial act is performed by a person other than a person described in subsections A and B of this section, sufficient proof of the authority of the person to act exists if the secretary of state certifies to the official character of the person and to the person's authority to perform the notarial act.

D. The signature and title of a person performing a notarial act are prima facie evidence that the person is a person with the designated title and that the signature is genuine.

§41-323. Change of address; lost journal or seal; civil penalty

A. Within thirty days after the change of a notary's mailing, business or residential address, the notary shall deliver to the secretary of state, by certified mail or other means providing a receipt, a signed notice of the change that provides both the old and new addresses.

B. Within ten days after the loss or theft of an official journal or seal, the notary shall deliver to the secretary of state, by certified mail or other means providing a receipt, a signed notice of the loss or theft. The notary also shall inform the appropriate law enforcement agency in the case of theft.

C. If a notary fails to comply with subsection A or B, the notary has failed to fully and faithfully discharge the duties of a notary and the secretary of state may impose a civil penalty of twenty five dollars against the notary. The notary shall pay any civil penalty imposed by the secretary of state pursuant to this subsection BEFORE to the renewal of the notary's commission.

ARIZONA NOTARY LAW PRIMER

§ 41-324. Court reporters; notarial acts

A. Court reporters who administer oaths and affirmations in judicial proceedings are exempt from the provisions of this chapter other than section 41 315. Court reporters who are commissioned as notaries and who perform notarial acts outside of judicial proceedings are subject to all provisions of this chapter and of other laws of this state that regulate notaries public.

B. A court reporter who prepares a transcript of a judicial proceeding shall attach a certificate page to the transcript. On the certificate page, the court reporter shall attest to the fact that the reporter administered an oath or affirmation to each witness whose testimony appears in the transcript.

C. An affidavit of nonappearance that is prepared by a court reporter does not need to be witnessed by a notary.

§ 41-325. Evidence of authenticity of a notarial act performed in this state

A. The authenticity of the official notarial seal and signature of a notary may be evidenced by either:

1. A certificate of authority from the secretary of state authenticated as necessary.

2. An apostille from the secretary of state in the form prescribed by the Hague convention of October 5, 1961 abolishing the requirement of legalization of foreign public documents.

B. An apostille as specified by the Hague convention shall be attached to any document that requires authentication and that is sent to a nation that has signed and ratified this convention.

§ 41-326. Apostille

An apostille prescribed by the Hague convention, as cited in 28 United States Code in annotations to rule 44 of the federal rules of civil procedure, shall be in the form of a square with sides at least nine centimeters long and shall contain exactly the following wording:

Apostille
(Convention de la Haye du 5 Octobre 1961)

1. Country: _____
   This public document
2. Has been signed by _____
3. Acting in the capacity of _____
4. Bears the seal/stamp of _____

Certified

5. At _____
6. The _____
7. By _____
8. No. _____
9. Seal/stamp
10. Signature _____

§ 41-327. Surname change; notification; continuation of commission

A notary public who has a change of surname may continue to use the official seal and commission in the notary public's prior name until that commission expires. The notary shall sign the changed surname on the line that is designated for the notary public's signature on the notarial certificate. Immediately below that signature, the notary public shall sign the name under which the notary was commissioned. The notary public shall notify the secretary of state's office within thirty days of the notary's change of surname. Failure to notify the secretary of state of this change of surname is evidence of the notary's failure to fully and faithfully discharge the duties of a notary.

§ 41-328. Prohibited conduct; incomplete documents; signatures of relatives

A. A notary public shall not perform a jurat on a document that is incomplete. If a notary public is presented with a document that the notary knows from experience to be incomplete or if the document on its face is incomplete the notary public shall refuse to perform the jurat.

B. A notary public is an impartial witness and shall not notarize the notary's own signature or the signatures of any person who is related to the notary by marriage or adoption.

C. Subject to Section 41-320, a notary public shall not perform a notarization on a document if the notary is an officer of any named party, if the notary is a party to the document or if the notary will receive any direct material benefit from the transaction that is evidenced by the notarized document that exceeds in value the fees prescribed pursuant to Section 41-316.

§ 41-329. Notary public title; foreign language; violation; classification

A. Every notary public who is not an attorney who advertises, by any written or verbal means, the services of a notary public in a language other than English, with the exception of a single desk plaque, shall post or otherwise include with the advertisement a notice in English and the other language. The notice shall be of conspicuous size, if in writing, and shall state: "I am not an attorney and cannot give legal advice about immigration or any other legal matters."

B. A notary public who violates subsection A of this section is guilty of a class 6 felony and the notary public's commission shall be permanently revoked.

§ 41-330. Grounds for refusal, revocation or suspension of commission

A. The secretary of state may refuse to appoint any person as a notary public or may revoke or suspend the commission of any notary public for any of the following reasons:

1. Substantial and material misstatement or omission in the application for a notary public commission that is submitted to the secretary of state.

2. Conviction of a felony unless restored to civil rights, or of a lesser offense involving moral turpitude or of a nature that is incompatible with

the duties of a notary public. A conviction after a plea of no contest is deemed to be a conviction for purposes of this paragraph.

    3. Revocation, suspension, restriction or denial of a professional license if that action was for misconduct, dishonesty or any cause that substantially relates to the duties or responsibilities of a notary public.

    4. Failure to discharge fully and faithfully any of the duties or responsibilities required of a notary public.

    5. The use of false or misleading advertising in which the notary public has represented that the notary public has duties, rights or privileges that the notary public does not possess by law.

    6. Charging more than the fees authorized by statute or rule.

    7. The commission of any act involving dishonesty, fraud or deceit with the intent to substantially benefit the notary public or another person or to substantially injure another person.

    8. Failure to complete the acknowledgment or jurat at the time the notary's signature and seal are affixed to the document.

    9. Failure to administer the oath or affirmation required at the time of performing a jurat for an individual.

    10. Execution of any notarial certificate by the notary public containing a statement known by the notary public to be false.

    11. The return for insufficient funds or any other reason for nonpayment of a check issued for the bond filing fees or the application fees to the secretary of state.

    12. Notarizing a document that contains no notarial certificate.

    B. If an application is denied the secretary of state shall notify the applicant within thirty days after receipt of the application and shall state the reasons for the denial.

    C. The secretary of state may suspend the commission of a notary for at least thirty days and for not more than one hundred eighty days.

    D. If a person has had a notary commission in this state revoked, the secretary of state may refuse to again appoint the person as a notary public for an indefinite period of time.

    E. On revocation or suspension of a notary public's commission, the secretary of state shall give notice to the notary public and shall provide the person with notice of the opportunity for a hearing on the revocation or suspension pursuant to chapter 6, article 10 of this title. The revocation or suspension of a notary public commission is an appealable agency action.

§ 41-331. Complaints; investigations

    A. Any person may make a complaint to the office of the secretary of state regarding a notary public. The secretary of state shall receive any complaints and shall provide notice of those complaints to the office of the attorney general who shall investigate and take action on all complaints involving allegations of any violations of this article.

    B. A notary's failure to respond to an investigation is a failure by the notary to fully and faithfully discharge the responsibilities and duties of a notary.

§ 41-332. Notary education fund

The notary education fund is established consisting of monies deposited pursuant to Sections 41-312 and 41-353. The secretary of state shall administer the fund. Monies in the fund are subject to legislative appropriation.

Title 41. State Government
Chapter 2. Administrative Officers
Article 3. Electronic Notarization

§ 41-351. Definitions

In this article, unless the context otherwise requires:

1. "Approved time stamp provider" means a person or organization recognized by the secretary of state as capable of reliably providing time stamp services on notary service electronic documents.

2. "Electronic" means relating to technology having electrical, digital, magnetic, wireless, optical, electromagnetic or similar capabilities.

3. "Electronic acknowledgment" means a notarial act in which an electronic notary electronically certifies that the signer, whose identity is proven by satisfactory evidence, either:

    (a) Appeared before the electronic notary and acknowledged that the signer executed the instrument.

    (b) Provided secure electronic acknowledgment that the signer executed the electronic instrument presented to the electronic notary.

4. "Electronic commission" means the written authority to perform electronic notarization acts.

5. "Electronic document" means any record created, generated, sent, communicated, received or stored by electronic means.

6. "Electronic jurat" means an electronic notarial act in which the electronic notary certifies that a signer, whose identity is proven by satisfactory evidence, has made in the electronic notary's presence a voluntary electronic signature or mark and has taken an oath or affirmation vouching for the truthfulness of the signed electronic document.

7. "Electronic notary public" or "electronic notary" means any person commissioned to perform notarial acts under this article.

8. "Electronic notary token" means the electronic attachment to a notarized electronic document that is attached by the electronic notary and that contains the notary's electronic signature. The electronic notary token is linked to the electronic document to which it relates in a manner so that if the document is changed the electronic notary token is invalidated.

9. "Electronic signature" means an electronic method or process that through the application of a security procedure allows a determination that the electronic signature at the time it was executed was all of the following:

    (a) Unique to the person using it.

    (b) Capable of verification.

    (c) Under the sole control of the person using it.

    (d) Linked to the electronic document to which it relates in a manner so that if the document is changed the electronic signature is invalidated.

10. "Notary service electronic certificate" means the materials and

ARIZONA NOTARY LAW PRIMER

methods issued by an electronic notary to a prospective signer so that signer may create a notary service electronic signature.

11. "Notary service electronic signature" means an act completed by a signer using a properly issued notary service electronic certificate to sign an electronic document.

12. "Oath" or "affirmation" means an act in which a person makes a vow in the presence of the electronic notary under penalty of perjury, with reference made to a supreme being in the case of an oath.

13. "Personal knowledge" means familiarity with an individual resulting from interactions with that individual over a sufficient time to eliminate reasonable doubt that the individual has the identity claimed.

14. "Satisfactory evidence of identity" means:

(a) Proof of identity is evidenced by one of the following:

(i) An unexpired driver license that is issued by a state or territory of the United States.

(ii) An unexpired passport that is issued by the United States department of state.

(iii) An unexpired identification card that is issued by any branch of the United States armed forces.

(iv) Any other unexpired identification card that is issued by the united states government or a state or tribal government, that contains the individual's photograph, signature and physical description and that contains the individual's height, weight, color of hair and color of eyes.

(v) The oath or affirmation of a credible person who is personally known to the electronic notary and who personally knows the individual signer.

(vi) The oath or affirmation of a credible person who personally knows the individual and who provides satisfactory evidence of identity pursuant to item (i), (ii), (iii) or (iv) of this subdivision (vii) Personal knowledge of the individual signer by the electronic notary.

(b) In addition to subdivision (a) of this paragraph, for the purposes of a real estate conveyance or financing, proof of identity may be evidenced by one of the following:

(i) A valid unexpired passport that is issued by the United States government.

(ii) A valid unexpired passport that is issued by a national government other than the United States government and that is accompanied by a valid unexpired visa or other documentation that is issued by the United States government and that is necessary to establish an individual's legal presence in the United States.

(iii) Any other valid unexpired identification that is deemed acceptable by the United States department of Homeland Security to establish an individual's legal presence in the United States and that is accompanied with supporting documents as required by the United States Department of Homeland Security.

15. "Time stamp token" means a secure electronic method to affix a statement of the time and date that the document was recognized as a valid notary service electronic document by an approved time stamp provider. A time stamp token is attached by an approved time stamp provider to the

document in a way that if the document changes the time stamp token is invalidated.

§ 41-352. Applicability of article; electronic signature laws

A. Any notarial act in which a person by oath or affirmation signs a document may be performed electronically as prescribed by this article if under applicable law that document may be signed with an electronic signature.

B. Unless otherwise expressly prohibited by law, the following notarial acts, terms and entities have the same legal effect as those prescribed by article 2 of this chapter:
1. Electronic acknowledgment as acknowledgment.
2. Electronic oath as oath.
3. Electronic jurat as jurat.
4. Electronic affidavit as affidavit.
5. Electronic notarial act as notarial act.
6. Electronic notarial certificate token as notarial certificate.
7. Electronic notary as notary.

C. An electronic commission is a commission to perform only electronic notary acts And only an electronic notary is authorized to perform electronic notary acts.

D. Unless otherwise expressly prohibited by law, any electronic notarial act may be performed by either:
1. An act in the presence of an electronic notary as prescribed by this article.
2. An electronic notarial service as prescribed by this article for which the person signing appears before an electronic notary and by oath or affirmation acknowledges that any notary service electronic document that is created by the person pursuant to this article has the same legal force and effect as if the person appeared before an electronic notary and by oath or affirmation executed an electronic notarial act.

E. Section 41-132 applies in conjunction with this article to electronic signatures used by electronic notaries.

F. This article applies to electronic notarial acts that are performed by electronic notaries who are appointed in this state and applies only to their acts performed in the United States.

§ 41-353. Appointment; term; bond; duties

A. The secretary of state may appoint electronic notaries public to hold office for four years.

B. The secretary of state shall prescribe the application form for an electronic notary. Applicants shall submit the application to the secretary of state with a filing fee, a bond and a bond filing fee as prescribed by rule by the secretary of state.

C. The materials and methods for creating notary service electronic certificates and any other encryption based technologies used by an electronic notary shall have a maximum useful life of two years and shall not exceed the life of the electronic notary commission.

D. An electronic notary public is a public officer commissioned by this

ARIZONA NOTARY LAW PRIMER

state and the following apply without regard to whether the electronic notary public's employer or any other person has paid the fees and costs for the commissioning of the electronic notary public, including costs for the materials and methods employed with the electronic notary token and the materials and methods for creating notary service electronic certificates and journals:

1. All of the following remain the property of the electronic notary:
   (a) The materials and methods employed with and solely for the electronic notary token.
   (b) The materials and methods used solely for creating notary service electronic certificates.
   (c) Any journals containing only public information record entries.

2. Notwithstanding paragraph 1 of this subsection, an electronic notary does not gain ownership or presumptive access rights to any of an employer's assets or resources that are used or are usable for a purpose other than electronic notarial acts.

3. An electronic notary may perform electronic notarizations outside the workplace of the electronic notary's employer except during those times normally designated as the electronic notary's hours of duty for that employer. All fees received by an electronic notary for electronic notarial services provided while not on duty remain the property of the electronic notary.

4. An employer of an electronic notary shall not limit the electronic notary's services to customers or other persons designated by the employer.

E. An electronic notary public shall continue to serve until the electronic notary's commission expires, the electronic notary resigns the commission, the electronic notary dies or the secretary of state suspends or revokes the commission. An employer shall not cancel the electronic notary bond or electronic notary commission of any electronic notary who is an employee and who leaves that employment.

F. An electronic notary shall comply with all of the following:

1. Be at least eighteen years of age.
2. Be a citizen or a legal permanent resident of the United States.
3. Be a resident of this state for income tax purposes and claim the individual's residence in this state as the individual's primary residence on state and federal tax returns.
4. Except as provided in section 41 368, subsection A, paragraph 2, never have been convicted of a felony.
5. Keep as a reference a manual that is approved by the secretary of state and that describes the duties, authority and ethical responsibilities of electronic notaries public.
6. Be able to read and write English.

G. An applicant for appointment and commission as an electronic notary shall complete an application form prescribed by the secretary of state. Except for the applicant's name, physical business address, electronic business address and business telephone number, all other information on the application is confidential and shall not be disclosed to any person other than the applicant, the applicant's personal representative or an officer or employee of the federal government or this state or its political subdivisions who is acting in an official capacity. The secretary of state shall use the information contained on the application only for carrying out the purposes of this article.

H. The state or any of its political subdivisions may pay the fees and costs for the commissioning of an electronic notary who is an employee of this state or any of its political subdivisions and performs electronic notarial services in the course of the electronic notary's employment or for the convenience of public employees.

I. The Secretary of State may require that applicants and suspended Notaries present proof of attendance at a Notary training course before receiving their commissions or before reinstatement of a suspended commission. Notaries shall attend a Notary training course within ninety days before renewing their commisions. The Secretary of State may assess a fee prescribed by the Secretary of State for administering notary training courses. The Secretary of State shall deposit the fees collected in the Notary Education Fund established by Section 41-332.

§ 41-354. Notarized electronic documents; elements

A. A notarized electronic document consists of the following:

1. A complete electronic document.

2. A signature or mark that is affixed to the document by the signer.

3. A time and date statement that is affixed to the document in a manner that is approved by the secretary of state.

4. An electronic notary token that is affixed to the document in a manner that is approved by the secretary of state.

B. On completion of the notarized electronic document, any change to any of the elements prescribed in subsection A invalidates the notarized electronic document.

§ 41-355. Duties; electronic notarization in presence of electronic notary

A. Electronic notaries public shall perform the following electronic notarial acts when requested:

1. Take electronic acknowledgments.

2. Administer oaths and affirmations relating to electronic documents and electronic notarial acts.

3. Perform jurats relating to electronic documents and electronic notarial acts.

B. Notaries public shall perform the notarial acts prescribed in Subsection A of this section only if:

1. The signer is in the presence of the notary at the time of notarization.

2. The signer signs in a language that the notary understands.

3. Subject to Subsection D, the signer communicates directly with the notary in a language they both understand or indirectly through a translator who is physically present with the signer and notary at the time of the notarization and communicates directly with the signer and the notary in languages the translator understands.

4. The notarial certificate is worded and completed using only letters, characters and a language that are read, written and understood by the notary public.

C. If a notary attaches a notarial certificate to a document using a separate sheet of paper, the attachment must contain a description of the document that includes at a minimum the title or type of document, the document date, the number of pages of the document and any additional signers other than those named in the notarial certificate.

D. A notary may perform a notarial act on a document that is a translation of a document that is in a language that the notary does not understand only if the person performing the translation signs an affidavit containing an oath or affirmation that the translation is accurate and complete. The notarized translation and affidavit shall be attached to the document and shall contain all of the elements described in Subsection C.

E. A notarized electronic document that is completed in the presence of an electronic notary consists of the following:

1. A complete electronic document.

2. A signature or mark that is affixed to the document by the signer.

3. A time and date statement that is contained within the electronic notary token.

4. An electronic notary token that is affixed by the electronic notary to the document.

F. On completion of the notarized electronic document, any change to any of the elements prescribed in subsection E of this section invalidates the notarized electronic document.

G. An electronic notary public shall:

1. Keep, maintain and protect as a public record a journal of all official acts performed by the notary as prescribed in section 41-361 and in the form prescribed by the secretary of state.

2. Provide and keep the materials and processes to create an electronic notary token as approved by the secretary of state.

3. Authenticate with the electronic notary token all official acts and affix the date of the expiration of the notary's commission as an electronic notary on every document that the electronic notary electronically signs.

4. Respond to any requests for information and comply with any investigations that are initiated by the secretary of state or the office of the attorney general.

§41-356. This section has been repealed as of July 29, 2010.

§ 41-357. Bond

A. A person who has been commissioned as an electronic notary shall file an oath of office and a bond with the secretary of state. A licensed surety shall execute the bond. The bond is effective for four years beginning on the commission's effective date.

B. The secretary of state shall not accept any bond that was issued more than sixty days before or more than thirty days after the date on which the secretary of state commissions an electronic notary.

§ 41-358. Fees; rules

A. Electronic notaries public may receive fees for the following services:

1. Acknowledgments.

2. Oaths and affirmations.
3. Jurats.
4. Issuance of notary service electronic certificates.

B. The secretary of state shall determine by rule fees for services.

C. A notary shall not advertise, charge or receive a fee for performing an electronic notarial act except as specifically authorized by rule.

§ 41-359. Delivering notarial journals and records; failure to comply; civil penalty; storing records; certified copies

A. On the resignation or revocation of an electronic notarial commission, the death of a notary or the expiration of an electronic commission, the electronic notarial journal and records, except those records of notarial acts that are not public record, shall be delivered by certified mail or other means providing a receipt to the office of the secretary of state. If an electronic notary does not apply for reappointment, on expiration of the notarial commission the journal and records shall be delivered to the secretary of state as required for resignation under this subsection. If an electronic notary or the personal representative of a deceased electronic notary does not deposit these records and papers within three months of the expiration of the commission, the secretary of state shall order the notary or the notary's personal representative to pay a civil penalty of at least fifty dollars but not more than five hundred dollars.

B. While an electronic notary public is commissioned, an electronic notary public shall keep all records and journals of the notary's acts for at least five years after the date the electronic notarial act was performed. On receipt of the records and journals from an electronic notary public who no longer is commissioned, the secretary of state shall keep all records and journals of electronic notaries public deposited in the secretary of state's office for five years and shall give certified copies when required, and for the copy certifications the secretary of state shall receive the same fees allowed by law to electronic notaries public pursuant to section 41-358. The copy certifications are as valid and effective as if given by an electronic notary public.

§ 41-360. Destruction of records; penalty

Any person who knowingly destroys, defaces or conceals any journal entry or records belonging to the office of an electronic notary public shall forfeit to the state not more than five hundred dollars and is liable for damages to any injured party.

§ 41-361. Journal; confidential records

A. The electronic notary shall keep or shall contract with a party that complies with procedures established by the secretary of state to keep a journal in a form approved by the secretary of state. The electronic notary shall record all notarial acts in chronological order. The electronic notary shall furnish, when requested, a certified copy of any specific public record in the notary's journal. Records of notarial acts that violate the attorney-client privilege or that are confidential pursuant to federal law or the laws of this state are not public record. Each journal entry shall include at least:

ARIZONA NOTARY LAW PRIMER

1. The date of the electronic notarial act.
2. A description of the document date, time and type of electronic notarial act.
3. The full name and address of each person for whom an electronic notarial act is performed and a description of the verification of the signer's mark.
4. The type of satisfactory evidence of identity presented to the electronic notary by each person for whom an electronic notarial act is performed.
5. A description of the identification document, its serial or identification number and its date of issuance or expiration.
6. The fee, if any, charged for the electronic notarial act.

B. If an electronic notary has personal knowledge of the identity of a signer, the requirements of subsection A, paragraphs 1 through 5 may be satisfied by the notary retaining a paper or electronic copy of the electronic notarized documents for each electronic notarial act.

C. If an electronic notary does more than one notarization for an individual within a six month period, the electronic notary shall have the individual provide satisfactory evidence of identity the first time the electronic notary performs the notarization for the individual but need not require satisfactory evidence of identity or the individual to sign the journal for subsequent notarizations performed for the individual during the six month period.

D. Except as provided in subsection A, the electronic notary's journal is a public record that may be viewed by or copied for any member of the public, but only on presentation to the notary of a written request that details the month and year of the electronic notarial act, the name of the person whose signature was notarized and the type of document or transaction. An electronic notary shall provide a copy of the requested entry in a form the secretary of state prescribes by rule.

§ 41-362. Competency of corporation notaries

A. An electronic notary public who is a stockholder, director, officer or employee of a corporation may do any of the following:
1. Take the acknowledgment or oath of any party to any written instrument executed to or by the corporation.
2. Administer an oath to any other stockholder, director, officer, employee or agent of the corporation.
3. Protest for nonacceptance or nonpayment of bills of exchange, drafts, checks, notes and other negotiable instruments that the corporation owns or holds for collection.

B. An electronic notary public shall not do any of the following:
1. Take the acknowledgment of an instrument executed by or to a corporation of which the electronic notary is a stockholder, director, officer or employee, if the notary is a party to the instrument, either individually or as a representative of the corporation.
2. Protest any negotiable instrument that the corporation owns or holds for collection, if the notary is individually a party to the instrument.

§ 41-363. Authentication of authority of officer for foreign notarizations

An electronic notarial act performed by any of the persons described in

§ 41-364. Change of address; lost or stolen electronic journal or seal; civil penalty

A. Within thirty days after the change of an electronic notary's mailing, business, residential or electronic address, the electronic notary shall deliver to the secretary of state, by certified mail or other means providing a receipt, a signed notice of the change that provides both the old and new addresses.

B. Within ten days after the loss or theft of an official journal or any materials or processes used in creating an electronic notary token or registering notary service electronic certificate applicants, the electronic notary shall deliver to the secretary of state, by certified mail or other means providing a receipt, a signed notice of the loss or theft. The electronic notary also shall inform the appropriate law enforcement agency in the case of theft.

C. If an electronic notary fails to comply with subsection A or B, the electronic notary has failed to fully and faithfully discharge the duties of an electronic notary and the secretary of state may impose against the electronic notary a civil penalty in an amount the secretary of state prescribes by rule. The electronic notary shall pay any civil penalty imposed by the secretary of state pursuant to this subsection before the renewal of the notary's commission.

§ 41-365. Name change; new commission; failure to comply

A. An electronic notary whose name changes shall apply for new methods and materials issued to the electronic notary to create electronic notary tokens under the new name.

B. An electronic notary shall notify the secretary of state within thirty days after the notary's change of name. If the electronic notary fails to comply with this subsection, the electronic notary has failed to fully and faithfully discharge the duties of an electronic notary.

§ 41-366. Prohibited conduct; incomplete documents; signatures of relatives

A. An electronic notary public shall not perform an electronic jurat on a document that is incomplete. If an electronic notary public is presented with a document that the electronic notary knows from experience to be incomplete or if the document on its face is incomplete, the electronic notary public shall refuse to perform the jurat.

B. An electronic notary public is an impartial witness and shall not notarize the notary's own signature or the signatures of any person who is related to the electronic notary by marriage or adoption.

C. Subject to Section 41-362, a Notary Public shall not perform a notarization on a document if the Notary is an officer of any named party, if the Notary is a party to the document or if the Notary will receive any direct material benefit from the transaction that is evidenced by the notarized document that exceeds in value the fees prescribed in Section 41-358.

§ 41-367. Electronic notary public title; foreign language; violation; classification

A. Every electronic notary public who is not an attorney and who advertises, by any written or verbal means, the services of an electronic notary public in a language other than English, with the exception of a single desk plaque, shall post or otherwise include with the advertisement a notice in English and the other language. The notice shall be in of conspicuous size, if in writing, and shall state: "I am not an attorney and cannot give legal advice about immigration or any other legal matters."

B. An electronic notary public who violates subsection A is guilty of a class 6 felony and the secretary of state shall permanently revoke the electronic notary public's commission.

§ 41-368. Grounds for refusal, suspension or revocation of commission

A. The secretary of state may refuse to appoint any person as an electronic notary public or may suspend or revoke the commission of any electronic notary public for any of the following reasons:

1. Substantial and material misstatement or omission in the application for an electronic notary public commission that is submitted to the secretary of state.

2. Conviction of a felony unless restored to civil rights, or of a lesser offense involving moral turpitude or of a nature that is incompatible with the duties of an electronic notary public. A conviction after a plea of no contest is deemed to be a conviction for purposes of this paragraph.

3. Revocation, suspension, restriction or denial of a professional license if that action was for misconduct, dishonesty or any cause that substantially relates to the duties or responsibilities of an electronic notary public.

4. Failure to discharge fully and faithfully any of the duties or responsibilities required of an electronic notary public.

5. The use of false or misleading advertising in which the electronic notary public has represented that the electronic notary public has duties, rights or privileges that the electronic notary public does not possess by law.

6. Charging more than the fees authorized by statute or rule.

7. The commission of any act involving dishonesty, fraud or deceit with the intent to substantially benefit the electronic notary public or another person or to substantially injure another person.

8. Failure to complete the electronic acknowledgment or electronic jurat at the time the electronic notary's signature and seal are affixed to the document.

9. Failure to administer the oath or affirmation required at the time of performing an electronic jurat for an individual.

10. Execution of any electronic notarial certificate by the electronic notary public containing a statement known by the electronic notary public to be false.

11. The return for insufficient funds or any other reason for nonpayment of a check issued for fees to the secretary of state.

12. Notarizing a document that does not contain a notarial certificate.

B. If an application is denied, the secretary of state shall notify the applicant within thirty days after receipt of the application and shall state the reasons for the denial.

C. The secretary of state may suspend the commission of an electronic notary for at least thirty days and for not more than one hundred eighty days.

D. If a person has had an electronic notary commission in this state revoked, the secretary of state may refuse to appoint the person as an electronic notary for four years after the date of the revocation.

E. On revocation or suspension of an electronic notary public's commission, the secretary of state shall give notice to the electronic notary public and shall provide the person with notice of the opportunity for a hearing on the revocation or suspension pursuant to chapter 6, article 10 of this title. The revocation or suspension of an electronic notary public commission is an appealable agency action.

§ 41-369. Duties of secretary of state

The secretary of state shall adopt rules pursuant to chapter 6 of this title that establish policies, procedures, fees and any other duties or services required by this article.

§ 41-370. Complaints; investigations; failure to respond

A. Any person may make a complaint to the office of the secretary of state regarding an electronic notary. The secretary of state shall receive any complaints and shall provide notice of those complaints to the office of the attorney general. The office of attorney general shall investigate and take action on all complaints involving any allegation of a violation of this article.

B. An electronic notary's failure to respond to an investigation is a failure by the notary to fully and faithfully discharge the responsibilities and duties of an electronic notary.

Title 10. Corporations and Associations
Chapter 19. Corporations and Associations Not for Profit
Article 2. Electric Cooperative Non Profit Membership Corporations

§ 10-2082. Taking of acknowledgments by officer or member

A person authorized to take acknowledgments under the laws of this state shall not be disqualified from taking acknowledgments of instruments executed in favor of a cooperative or to which it is a party, by reason of being an officer, director or member of the cooperative.

Title 12. Courts and Civil Proceedings
Chapter 2. Judicial Officers and Employees
Article 8. Clerk of the Superior Court

§ 12-284. Fees

A. Except as otherwise provided by law, the clerk of the superior court shall receive fees classified as follows:

Class	Description	Fee
G	Special fees	
	Notary services	7.00

Title 14. Decedents' Estates and Protective Proceedings
Chapter 5. Protection of Persons Under Disability and Their Property
Article 5. Powers of Attorney

§ 14-5501. Durable power of attorney; creation; validity

A. A durable power of attorney is a written instrument by which a principal designates another person as the principal's agent. The instrument shall contain words that demonstrate the principal's intent that the authority conferred in the durable power of attorney may be exercised:

1. If the principal is subsequently disabled or incapacitated.

2. Regardless of how much time has elapsed, unless the instrument states a definite termination time.

B. The written instrument may demonstrate the principal's intent required by subsection A of this section using either of the following statements or similar language:

1. "This power of attorney is not affected by subsequent disability or incapacity of the principal or lapse of time."

2. "This power of attorney is effective on the disability or incapacity of the principal."

C. A power of attorney executed in another jurisdiction of the United States is valid in this state if the power of attorney was validly executed in the jurisdiction in which it was created.

D. Except as provided in section 28-370, an adult, known as the principal, may designate another adult, known as the agent, to make financial decisions on the principal's behalf by executing a written power of attorney that satisfies all of the following requirements:

1. Contains language that clearly indicates that the principal intends to create a power of attorney and clearly identifies the agent.

2. Is signed or marked by the principal or signed in the principal's name by some other individual in the principal's conscious presence and at the principal's direction.

3. Is witnessed by a person other than the agent, the agent's spouse, the agent's children or the notary public.

4. Is executed and attested by its acknowledgment by the principal and by an affidavit of the witness before a notary public and evidenced by the notary public's certificate, under official seal, in substantially the following form:

> I, _____, the principal, sign my name to this power of attorney this _____ day of _____ and, being first duly sworn, do declare to the undersigned authority that I sign and execute this instrument as my power of attorney and that I sign it willingly, or willingly direct another to sign for me, that I execute it as my free and voluntary act for the purposes expressed in the power of attorney and that I am eighteen years of age or older, of sound mind and under no constraint or undue influence.

Principal
I, _____, the witness, sign my name to the foregoing power of attorney being first duly sworn and do declare to the undersigned authority that the principal signs and executes this instrument as the principal's power of attorney and that the principal signs it willingly, or willingly directs another to sign for the principal, and that I, in the presence and hearing of the principal, sign this power of attorney as witness to the principal's signing and that to the best of my knowledge the principal is eighteen years of age or older, of sound mind and under no constraint or undue influence.

_____
Witness
The state of _____
County of _____
Subscribed, sworn to and acknowledged before me by _____, the principal, and subscribed and sworn to before me by _____, witness, this _____ day of _____.
(seal)
(signed) _____

_____
(notary public)

E. The execution requirements for the creation of a power of attorney provided in subsection D of this section do not apply if the principal creating the power of attorney is:

1. A person other than a natural person.

2. Any person, if the power of attorney to be created is a power coupled with an interest. For the purposes of this paragraph, "power coupled with an interest" means a power that forms a part of a contract and is security for money or for the performance of a valuable act.

F. A person whose license as a fiduciary has been suspended or revoked pursuant to section 14-5651 may not serve as an agent under a power of attorney in any capacity unless the person is related to the principal by blood, adoption or marriage. This prohibition does not apply if the person's license has been reinstated and is in good standing.

Title 16. Elections and Electors
Chapter 5. Political Parties
Article 2. Party Organization and Government

§ 16-828. Proxies

A. A political party may choose, through its bylaws, to allow the use of proxies at its meetings, in which event the following shall be minimum regulations:

1. No proxy shall be given by a member of the state committee for use at a meeting of the committee except to a qualified elector of the county where the member resides.

2. No proxy shall be given by a member of the county committee for use at a meeting of the committee except to a qualified elector of the precinct where the member resides.

B. The duration of any proxy so given shall extend only for the length of the meeting for which it is given.

C. Every proxy shall be attested by a notary public or two witnesses.

Title 26. Military Affairs and Emergency Management
Chapter 1. Emergency and Military Affairs
Article 3. National Guard

§ 26-160. Oaths or affirmations

Oaths or affirmations required in the military service shall be administered by any commissioned officer, or other officer authorized to administer oaths, and no charge shall be made therefor.

Title 33. Property
Chapter 4. Conveyances and Deeds
Article 5. Uniform Recognition of Acknowledgments Act

§ 33-501. Recognition of notarial acts performed outside this state

For the purposes of this article, "notarial acts" means acts which the laws and regulations of this state authorize notaries public of this state to perform, including the administering of oaths and affirmations, taking proof of execution and acknowledgments of instruments, and attesting documents. Notarial acts may be performed outside this state for use in this state with the same effect as if performed by a notary public of this state by the following persons authorized pursuant to the laws and regulations of other governments in addition to any other person authorized by the laws and regulations of this state:

1. A notary public authorized to perform notarial acts in the place in which the act is performed.

2. A judge, clerk, or deputy clerk of any court of record in the place in which the notarial act is performed.

3. An officer of the foreign service of the United States, a consular agent, or any other person authorized by regulation of the United States department of state to perform notarial acts in the place in which the act is performed.

4. A commissioned officer in active service with the armed forces of the United States and any other person authorized by regulation of the armed forces to perform notarial acts if the notarial act is performed for one of the following or his dependents: a merchant seaman of the United States, a member of the armed forces of the United States, or any other person serving with or accompanying the armed forces of the United States.

5. Any other person authorized to perform notarial acts in the place in which the act is performed.

§ 33-502. Authentication of authority of officer

A. If the notarial act is performed by any of the persons described in section 33-501, paragraphs 1 through 4, inclusive, other than a person authorized to perform notarial acts by the laws or regulations of a foreign country, the signature, rank, or title and serial number, if any, of the person are sufficient proof of the authority of a holder of that rank or title to perform the act. Further proof of his authority is not required.

B. If the notarial act is performed by a person authorized by the laws or regulations of a foreign country to perform the act, there is sufficient proof of the authority of that person to act if:

1. Either a foreign service officer of the United States resident in the country in which the act is performed or a diplomatic or consular officer of the foreign country resident in the United States certifies that a person holding that office is authorized to perform the act, or

2. The official seal of the person performing the notarial act is affixed to the document, or

3. The title and indication of authority to perform notarial acts of the person appears either in a digest of foreign law or in a list customarily used as a source of such information.

C. If the notarial act is performed by a person other than one described in subsections A and B, there is sufficient proof of the authority of that person to act if the secretary of state certifies to the official character of that person and to his authority to perform the notarial act.

D. The signature and title of the person performing the act are prima facie evidence that he is a person with the designated title and that the signature is genuine.

§ 33-503. Certificate of person taking acknowledgment

The person taking an acknowledgment shall certify that:

1. The person acknowledging appeared before him and acknowledged he executed the instrument, and

2. The person acknowledging was known to the person taking the acknowledgment or that the person taking the acknowledgment had satisfactory evidence that the person acknowledging was the person described in and who executed the instrument.

§ 33-504. Recognition of certificate of acknowledgment

The form of a certificate of acknowledgment used by a person whose authority is recognized under section 33-501 shall be accepted in this state if:

1. The certificate is in a form prescribed by the laws or regulations of this state, or

2. The certificate is in a form prescribed by the laws or regulations applicable in the place in which the acknowledgment is taken, or

3. The certificate contains the words "acknowledged before me", or their substantial equivalent.

§ 33-505. Certificate of acknowledgment

The words "acknowledged before me" mean that:

1. The person acknowledging appeared before the person taking the acknowledgment.

2. He acknowledged he had executed the instrument.

3. In the case of:

(a) A natural person, he executed the instrument for the purposes therein stated.

ARIZONA NOTARY LAW PRIMER

(b) A corporation, the officer or agent acknowledged he held the position or title set forth in the instrument and certificate, he signed the instrument on behalf of the corporation by proper authority, and the instrument was the act of the corporation for the purpose therein stated.

(c) A partnership, the partner or agent acknowledged he signed the instrument on behalf of the partnership by proper authority and he executed the instrument as the act of the partnership for the purposes therein stated.

(d) A person acknowledging as principal by an attorney in fact, he executed the instrument by proper authority as the act of the principal for the purposes therein stated.

(e) A person acknowledging as a public officer, trustee, personal representative, administrator, guardian, or other representative, he signed the instrument by proper authority and he executed the instrument in the capacity and for the purposes therein stated.

4. The person taking the acknowledgment either knew or had satisfactory evidence that the person acknowledging was the person named in the instrument or certificate.

§ 33-506. Short forms of acknowledgment

The forms of acknowledgment set forth in this section may be used and are sufficient for their respective purposes under any law of this state. The forms shall be known as "statutory short forms of acknowledgment" and may be referred to by that name. The authorization of the following forms does not preclude the use of other forms:

1. For an individual acting in his own right:
    State of _____
    County of _____
    The foregoing instrument was acknowledged before me this (date) by (name of person acknowledged.)
    (Signature of person taking acknowledgment)
    (Title or rank)
    (Serial number, if any)

2. For a corporation:
    State of _____
    County of _____
    The foregoing instrument was acknowledged before me this (date) by (name of officer or agent, title or officer or agent) of (name of corporation acknowledging) a (state or place of incorporation) corporation, on behalf of the corporation.
    (Signature of person taking acknowledgment)
    (Title or rank)
    (Serial number, if any)

3. For a partnership:
    State of _____
    County of _____
    The foregoing instrument was acknowledged before me this (date) by (name of acknowledging partner or agent), partner (or agent) on behalf of (name of partnership), a partnership.
    (Signature of person taking acknowledgment)
    (Title or rank)
    (Serial number, if any)

4. For an individual acting as principal by an attorney in fact:
State of _____
County of _____
The foregoing instrument was acknowledged before me this (date) by (name of attorney in fact) as attorney in fact on behalf of (name of principal).
(Signature of person taking acknowledgment)
(Title or rank)
(Serial number, if any)
5. By any public officer, trustee, or personal representative:
State of _____
County of _____
The foregoing instrument was acknowledged before me this (date) by (name and title of position).
(Signature of person taking acknowledgment)
(Title or rank)
(Serial number, if any)

§ 33-507. Acknowledgments not affected by this article

A notarial act performed prior to the effective date of this article is not affected by this article. This article provides an additional method of proving notarial acts. Nothing in this article diminishes or invalidates the recognition accorded to notarial acts by other laws or regulations of this state.

§ 33-508. Uniformity of interpretation

This article shall be so interpreted as to make uniform the laws of those states which enact it.

Title 33. Property
Chapter 4. Conveyances and Deeds
Article 6. Acknowledgments

§ 33-511. Acknowledgment within the state

The acknowledgment of any instrument may be made in this state before:
1. A judge of a court of record.
2. A clerk or deputy clerk of a court having a seal.
3. A recorder of deeds.
4. A notary public.
5. A justice of the peace.
6. A county recorder.

§ 33-512. Acknowledgment by a married woman

An acknowledgment of a married woman may be made in the same form as though she were unmarried.

§ 33-513. Action to correct certificate of acknowledgment

When an acknowledgment is properly made, but defectively certified, any party interested may bring an action in the superior court to obtain a judgment correcting the certificate.

Title 36. Public Health and Safety
Chapter 20. Abortion
Article 1. General Provisions

§ 36-2152. Parental consent; exception; hearings; time limits; violation; classification; civil relief; statute of limitations

A. In addition to the requirements of section 36-2153, a person shall not knowingly perform an abortion on a pregnant unemancipated minor unless the attending physician has secured the written and notarized consent from one of the minor's parents or the minor's guardian or conservator or unless a judge of the superior court authorizes the physician to perform the abortion pursuant to subsection B of this section. Notwithstanding section 41-319, the notarized statement of parental consent and the description of the document or notarial act recorded in the notary journal are confidential and are not public records.

Title 38. Public Officers and Employees
Chapter 2. Qualification and Tenure
Article 4. Oath of Office

§ 38-233. Filing oaths of record

A. The official oaths of state elective officers shall be filed of record in the office of the secretary of state. The official oaths of all other state officers and employees shall be filed of record in the office of the employing state board, commission or agency.

B. The official oaths of elective county and elective precinct officers shall be filed of record in the office of the county recorder, except the oath of the recorder, which shall be filed with the clerk of the board of supervisors. The official oaths of notaries public shall be endorsed upon their bond and filed with the secretary of state. The official oaths of all other county and precinct officers and employees shall be filed of record in the office of the employing county or precinct board, commission or agency.

C. The official oaths of all city, town or municipal corporation officers or employees shall be filed of record in the respective office of the employing board, commission or agency of the cities, towns and municipal corporations.

D. The official oaths of all officers and employees of all school districts shall be filed of record in the school district office.

E. The official oaths of all officers and employees of each public educational institution except school districts shall be filed of record in the respective offices of the public educational institutions.

F. The official oath or affirmation required to be filed of record shall be maintained as an official record throughout the person's term, appointment or employment plus a period of time to be determined pursuant to sections 41-1347 and 41-1351.

Title 38. Public Officers and Employees
Chapter 2. Qualification and Tenure
Article 6. Vacancy in Office

§ 38-291. Vacancy defined

An office shall be deemed vacant from and after the occurrence of any of the following events before the expiration of a term of office:

1. Death of the person holding the office.
2. Insanity of the person holding the office, when judicially determined.
3. Resignation of the person holding the office and the lawful acceptance of the resignation.
4. Removal from office of the person holding the office.
5. If the office is elective, the person holding the office ceasing to be a resident of the state, or, if the office is local, or from a legislative or congressional district, the person holding the office ceasing to be a resident of the district, county, city, town or precinct for which he was elected, or within which the duties of his office are required to be discharged.
6. Absence from the state by the person holding the office, without permission of the legislature, beyond the period of three consecutive months.
7. The person holding the office ceasing to discharge the duties of office for the period of three consecutive months.
8. Conviction of the person holding the office of a felony or an offense involving a violation of his official duties.
9. Failure of the person elected or appointed to such office to file his official oath within the time prescribed by law.
10. A decision of a competent tribunal declaring void the election or appointment of the person elected or appointed to the office.
11. Failure of a person to be elected or appointed to the office.
12. A violation of section 38-296 by the person holding the office.

§ 38-294. Resignations

Resignations shall be in writing, and made as follows:

1. By members of the legislature, to the presiding officer of the body of which he is a member, who shall immediately transmit the resignation to the governor.
2. By state officers, notaries public and officers of the militia, to the governor.
3. By other officers commissioned by the governor, to the governor.
4. By county officers, to the chairman of the board of supervisors of their county.
5. By the chairman of the board of supervisors, to the county recorder of the county.
6. In cases not otherwise provided for, by filing the resignation in the office of the secretary of state.
7. By appointive officers, to the body or officer which appointed them, unless otherwise provided.

Title 38. Public Officers and Employees
Chapter 3. Conduct of Office
Article 2. Fees

§ 38-412. Posting schedule of fees
Recorders, clerks of the superior courts, sheriffs, justices of the peace, constables and notaries public shall keep posted at all times in a conspicuous place in their respective offices a complete list of the fees they are allowed to charge.

§ 38-413. Charging excessive fees; classification
A. If an officer demands and receives a higher fee than prescribed by law, or any fee not so allowed, such officer shall be liable to the party aggrieved in an amount four times the fee unlawfully demanded and received by him.
B. An officer who violates this section is guilty of a class 5 felony.

Title 38. Public Officers and Employees
Chapter 3. Conduct of Office
Article 3. Records

§ 38-423. Making or giving false certificate; classification
A public officer authorized by law to make or give any certificate or other writing, who makes and delivers as true such a certificate or writing containing a statement which he knows is false, is guilty of a class 6 felony.

Title 39. Public Records, Printing and Notices
Chapter 1. Public Notices
Article 2. Searches and Copies

§ 39-122. Free searches for and copies of public records to be used in claims against United States; liability for noncompliance
A. No state, county or city, or any officer or board thereof shall demand or receive a fee or compensation for issuing certified copies of public records or for making search for them, when they are to be used in connection with a claim for a pension, allotment, allowance, compensation, insurance or other benefits which is to be presented to the United States or a bureau or department thereof.
B. Notaries public shall not charge for an acknowledgment to a document which is to be so filed or presented.
C. The services specified in subsections A and B shall be rendered on request of an official of the United States, a claimant, his guardian or attorney. For each failure or refusal so to do, the officer so failing shall be liable on his official bond.

Title 39. Public Records, Printing and Notices
Chapter 1. Public Notices
Article 4. False Instruments and Records

§ 39-161. Presentment of false instrument for filing; classification

A person who acknowledges, certifies, notarizes, procures or offers to be filed, registered or recorded in a public office in this state an instrument he knows to be false or forged, which, if genuine, could be filed, registered or recorded under any law of this state or the United States, or in compliance with established procedure is guilty of a class 6 felony. As used in this section "instrument" includes a written instrument as defined in section 13-2001.

Title 41. State Government
Chapter 1. Executive Officers
Article 2. The Secretary of State and the Department of State

§ 41-126. Fees; expedited services

A. The secretary of state shall receive the following fees:

1. Making a copy of any document on file in his office, no more than ten cents for each page or partial page.

2. Filing and recording each application to become a notary public and transmitting a commission for a notary public, no more than twenty-five dollars.

10. Filing, recording or certifying any other document not specified in this section, no more than three dollars.

11. Filing the oath and bond of notary public, eighteen dollars.

12. Issuing a certificate as to official capacity of a notary public and affixing a seal to the certificate, eighteen dollars.

B. The secretary of state shall provide for and establish an expedited service for the processing of requests, applications, filings and searches as follows:

1. The expedited processing shall be a priority same day service effected in a fast and efficient manner.

2. A fee shall be charged for expedited services. This fee shall not exceed twenty-five dollars per service and shall be in addition to any other fees provided by law, including those set forth in subsection A of this section.

C. The secretary of state shall adopt rules necessary to carry out subsection B of this section.

Title 42. Taxation
Chapter 11. Property Tax
Article 4. Qualifying For Exemptions

§ 42-11152. Affidavit; false statements

A. Except as provided in sections 42-11104, 42-11109, 42-11110, 42-11111 and 42-11131 and except for property described in sections 42-11125, 42-11127 and 42-11132, a person who claims exemption from taxation under article IX, section 2, 2.1 or 2.2, Constitution of Arizona, shall:

ARIZONA NOTARY LAW PRIMER

1. When initially claiming the exemption, appear before the county assessor to make an affidavit as to the person's eligibility. If a personal appearance before the county assessor would create a severe hardship, the county assessor may arrange a mutually satisfactory meeting place to make an affidavit as to the person's eligibility.

2. When claiming the exemption in subsequent years, appear before the county assessor or a notary public to make an affidavit as to the person's eligibility.

3. Fully answer all questions on the eligibility form or otherwise required by the assessor for that purpose.

B. At the assessor's discretion, the assessor may require additional proof of the facts stated by the person before allowing an exemption.

C. A person who is in the United States military service and who is absent from this state or who is confined in a veterans' hospital or another licensed hospital may make the required affidavit in the presence of any officer who is authorized to administer oaths on a form obtained from the county assessor.

D. A false statement that is made or sworn to in the affidavit is perjury.

ARIZONA ADMINISTRATIVE CODE
Title 2. Administration
Chapter 12. Office of the Secretary of State
Article 11. Notary Public Bonds and Fees

R2-12-1101. Definitions

The following definitions shall apply in this Article unless the context otherwise requires:

"Acknowledgment" means the same as defined in A.R.S. § 41-311(1).

"Bond" means a surety bond to the state, with sureties approved by the clerk of the superior court in the county in which the individual is being commissioned as a notary public.

"Copy certification" means the same as defined in A.R.S. § 41-311(3).

"Credible person" means a person used to identify a signer when the signer does not have other satisfactory evidence of identity as specified in A.R.S. § 41-311(11).

"Jurat" means the same as defined in A.R.S. § 41-311(6).

"Oath" or "affirmation" means the same as defined in A.R.S. § 41-311(10).

"Satisfactory evidence of identity" means the same as defined in A.R.S. § 41-311(11).

Historical Note

New Section adopted by emergency rulemaking at 6 A.A.R. 2956, effective July 18, 2000 (Supp. 00-3). Emergency rulemaking renewed at 7 A.A.R. 672, effective January 13, 2001 (Supp. 01-1). Section made by final rulemaking at 7 A.A.R. 2141, effective May 1, 2001 (Supp. 01-2).

R2-12-1102. Notary Public Fees

Notaries public may charge the following fees:

1. For acknowledgments, $2 per signature;
2. For jurats, $2 per signature;
3. For copy certifications, $2 per page certified;
4. For oaths or affirmations without a signature, $2.

Historical Note
New Section adopted by emergency rulemaking at 6 A.A.R. 2956, effective July 18, 2000 (Supp. 00-3). Emergency rulemaking renewed at 7 A.A.R. 672, effective January 13, 2001 (Supp. 01-1). Section made by final rulemaking at 7 A.A.R. 2141, effective May 1, 2001 (Supp. 01-2).

R2-12-1103. Notary Public Bonds
A. Notaries public shall purchase a bond in the amount of $5,000 before being commissioned as a notary public. The original bond shall be filed with the clerk of the superior court in the applicant's county of residence. A copy of the bond shall be filed with the applicant's application form submitted to the Secretary of State's Office.

B. The bond shall contain, on its face, the oath of office for the notary public as specified in A.R.S. § 38-233(B). This oath shall be as specified in A.R.S. § 38-231. The notary shall endorse the oath on the face of the bond, immediately below the oath, by signing the notary's name under which the person has applied to be commissioned as a notary and exactly as the name appears on the notary application form filed with the Secretary of State's Office.

Historical Note
New Section adopted by emergency rulemaking at 6 A.A.R. 2956, effective July 18, 2000 (Supp. 00-3). Emergency rulemaking renewed at 7 A.A.R. 672, effective January 13, 2001 (Supp. 01-1). Section made by final rulemaking at 7 A.A.R. 2141, effective May 1, 2001 (Supp. 01-2).

Title 2. Administration
Chapter 12. Secretary of State
Article 12. Electronic Notary

Article 12, consisting of Sections R2-12-1201 through R2-12-1209, made by final rulemaking at 9 A.A.R. 2085, effective August 1, 2003 (Supp. 03-2).

R2-12-1201. Application and Renewal
Each applicant for an electronic notary commission or a renewal of an electronic notary commission shall:
1. Submit to the Secretary of State a verified application on a form furnished by the Secretary of State that provides the following information about the applicant:
   a. Full name and any former names used by the applicant;
   b. Physical address and telephone number;
   c. Mailing address and telephone number;
   d. Business address, telephone number, fax number and email address, if applicable;
   e. County of residence;
   f. Gender;

g. Date of birth;
h. The previous commission number of the applicant if previously an electronic notary or notary public appointed under A.R.S. § 41-312 in Arizona, if applicable;
i. Responses to questions regarding the applicant's background on the following subjects:
  i. Whether the applicant has been convicted of a felony or an undesignated offense in this or any other jurisdiction and whether the applicant has been restored to civil rights.
  ii. Whether the applicant has been convicted of a lesser offense involving moral turpitude or of a nature that is incompatible with the duties of a notary public in this or any other jurisdiction such as a finding that the applicant engaged in conduct that would violate A.R.S. § 41-313 if adjudicated in Arizona, or that the applicant engaged in conduct that constituted misconduct in public office or demonstrated dishonesty or a lack of veracity.
  iii. Whether the applicant has ever had a professional license revoked, suspended, restricted, or denied for misconduct, dishonesty, or any cause that relates to the duties or responsibilities of a notary public such as a finding that the applicant engaged in conduct that would violate A.R.S. § 41-313 if adjudicated in Arizona, or that the applicant engaged in conduct that demonstrated dishonesty or a lack of veracity.
  iv. Whether the applicant has had a notary commission revoked, suspended, restricted, or denied in this state or any other jurisdiction.
  v. Statement that applicant is 18 years of age or older.
  vi. Statement of being an Arizona resident.
  vii. Whether the applicant holds or has held a notary commission in another state or jurisdiction and the commission number and jurisdiction, if applicable.
2. The Secretary of State may require that the applicant provide a detailed explanation and supporting documentation for each response on the application regarding the applicant's background.
3. Each applicant shall register with the Secretary of State the applicant's possession of an approved electronic notary token within 90 days of submitting the application.

Historical Note
New Section made by final rulemaking at 9 A.A.R. 2085, effective August 1, 2003 (Supp. 03-2).

R2-12-1202. Applicant Filing Fee, Bond, and Bond Filing Fee
A. The application and renewal fee is $25.
B. The bond filing fee is $25.
C. The applicant shall purchase a surety bond in the amount of $25,000. The original bond shall be filed with the Secretary of State's office accompanying the application or renewal.
D. The bond shall contain, on its face, the oath of office for the electronic notary public as specified in A.R.S. § 38-231(G). The electronic notary shall endorse the oath on the face of the bond, immediately below the oath, by signing the electronic notary's name under which the person has applied to be

ARIZONA LAWS PERTAINING TO NOTARIES PUBLIC

commissioned as an electronic notary and exactly as the name appears on the electronic notary application form filed with the Secretary of State's Office.

Historical Note
New Section made by final rulemaking at 9 A.A.R. 2085, effective August 1, 2003 (Supp. 03-2).

R2-12-1203. Notarial Journal

A. An electronic notary public shall keep a journal of all electronic notarial acts in bound paper form with the same form as required in A.R.S. § 41-319 herein referenced as a "journal." If an electronic notary act is conducted upon an electronic signature that is not recognized under A.R.S. § 41-132, the electronic notary shall have the signer sign the paper journal in a manner consistent with A.R.S. § 41-319.

B. The journal shall be under the control of the electronic notary.

C. If an electronic notary also holds commission as a notary public appointed under A.R.S. § 41-312, and the commission dates are identical between the two commissions, then the electronic notary may use the notary public journal as the electronic notary paper journal. If the dates are not identical, then the electronic notary shall maintain two separate journals.

D. If a notary service electronic certificate is used in a manner to create an electronic signature in a notarial act, the document name, title, brief description of contents, and the time stamp shall be entered into the issuing electronic notary's journal as a notary service electronic certificate entry.

E. Journals are not deemed received until the Secretary of State accepts the journals as complete. The electronic notary shall not be subject to a penalty for delay outside the control of the electronic notary in delivering the journal to the Secretary of State.

Historical Note
New Section made by final rulemaking at 9 A.A.R. 2085, effective August 1, 2003 (Supp. 03-2).

R2-12-1204. Standards for Electronic Notary Token and Notary Service Electronic Certificate

A. An electronic notary token, and subsequently a notary service electronic certificate, shall be approved under A.R.S. § 41-132.

B. A provider of an electronic notary token may not provide an official electronic notary token to a person unless the person first presents evidence of the electronic notary commission for that person to the provider.

C. A provider of a notary service electronic certificate may not provide an official notary service electronic certificate to a person unless the person presents himself or herself before and receives authorization from an electronic notary for reception of the notary service electronic certificate.

D. An electronic notary token shall contain:
1. The commission number of the electronic notary;
2. The full name of the electronic notary, as commissioned as an electronic notary;
3. The expiration date of the notary's commission;
4. A link to the commission record of the electronic notary on the

ARIZONA NOTARY LAW PRIMER

Secretary of State's official web site; and
    5. Any applicable information relative to A.R.S. § 41-132.
  E. A notary service electronic certificate shall contain:
    1. The commission number of the electronic notary authorizing the notary service electronic certificate;
    2. The identification of the authorizing electronic notary's electronic notary token;
    3. The full name of the individual, as presented to the electronic notary;
    4. A link to the authorizing commission record of the electronic notary on the Secretary of State's official web site; and
    5. Any applicable information relative to A.R.S. § 41-132.
  F. An electronic notary may possess only one electronic notary token.

Historical Note
New Section made by final rulemaking at 9 A.A.R. 2085, effective August 1, 2003 (Supp. 03-2).

R2-12-1205. Use of Electronic Notary Tokens and Notary Service Electronic Certificate

  A. An electronic notary may only use an electronic notary token for the duties set forth in A.R.S. §§ 41-351 through 41-369 and interactions with the provider of the electronic notary token.

  B. A person may only use a notary service electronic certificate for the purposes of creating electronic notarized documents and interactions with the provider of the notary service electronic certificate.

  C. Use of an electronic notary token is not complete without:
    1. Incorporating the electronic notary token elements into the document;
    2. Either directly incorporating the time and date of notarization or incorporating the time and date of notarization using a process of an approved time stamp provider;
    3. Affixing the notary's electronic signature.

  D. Use of a notary service electronic certificate is not complete without:
    1. Presence of a date and time stamp from an approved time stamp token provider;
    2. Affixing the notary's electronic signature.

Historical Note
New Section made by final rulemaking at 9 A.A.R. 2085, effective August 1, 2003 (Supp. 03-2).

R2-12-1206. Approval of Time Stamp Token Provider

Any person or entity that can provide a service that synchronizes time as defined in A.R.S. § 1-242 into a process using an electronic notary token or a notary service electronic certificate, where applicable, may be added to the list of approved time stamp token providers. All time stamp tokens that interact with electronic notary tokens and notary service electronic certificates need to meet the applicable technology standards required by A.R.S. § 41-132.

Historical Note
New Section made by final rulemaking at 9 A.A.R. 2085, effective August

1, 2003 (Supp. 03-2).

R2-12-1207. Fees
Electronic notaries may charge the following fees:
1. Fee for an acknowledgment shall be not more than $25.
2. Fee for an oath or affirmation shall be not more than $25.
3. Fee for a jurat shall be not more than $25.
4. Fee for authorizing a notary service electronic certificate to a person shall be not more than $50. This does not include any vendor fees or charges to the person for reception of the notary service electronic certificate.
5. Fee for any other notarial act shall be not more than $25.

Historical Note
New Section made by final rulemaking at 9 A.A.R. 2085, effective August 1, 2003 (Supp. 03-2).

R2-12-1208. Penalty Fee for Lack of Notice
The penalty to be imposed upon an electronic notary for failure to provide signed notice as defined in the statute to the Secretary of State of each loss, theft, or compromise of the electronic notary's journal shall be $10 per use of electronic notary token up to a maximum of $500. When audit trail is not recoverable, the maximum of $500 shall be imposed upon the electronic notary for each failure to provide proper notice of a loss, theft, or compromise of the electronic notary's journal.

Historical Note
New Section made by final rulemaking at 9 A.A.R. 2085, effective August 1, 2003 (Supp. 03-2).

R2-12-1209. Civil Penalties
A. The penalty to be imposed upon an electronic notary for failure to provide signed notice as defined in the statute to the Secretary of State of each loss, theft, or compromise of a notary service electronic certificate or of loss, theft or compromise of any materials or processes used in creating an electronic notary token or authorizing a notary service electronic certificate shall be $10 per day, up to a maximum of $500 for each failure to provide proper notice of a loss, theft, or compromise of a notary service electronic certificate or compromise of any materials or processes used in creating an electronic notary token.

B. The penalty to be imposed upon an electronic notary for each failure to provide signed notice as defined in the statute to the Secretary of State of a change of address shall be $10 per day, up to a maximum of $250 for each failure to provide proper notice of a change of address.

C. The penalty to be imposed upon an electronic notary for failure to deposit the notary's electronic notary journal and records as defined in the statute with the Secretary of State shall be $50 for the first day and then $10 per day up to a maximum of $500.

Historical Note
New Section made by final rulemaking at 9 A.A.R. 2085, effective August 1, 2003 (Supp. 03-2).

ATTORNEY GENERAL OPINIONS

Opinion I97-015 (R97-040), dated December 30, 1997
The Attorney General has held that the Secretary of State has the authority to revoke a notary public's commission, or to seek to remove a notary public from office, for cause as specified in State law, after notice and an opportunity for a hearing. The Legislature may, by statute, expressly grant the Secretary of State additional authority to regulate and remove notaries public from office.

Opinion I97-011 (R97-033), dated August 15, 1997
The Attorney General has held that notarial acts performed in Arizona under the authority of federal law for members of the armed forces and related eligible recipients of federal legal assistance are valid in Arizona. ■

Office of the Arizona Secretary of State

Arizona Secretary of State
Notary Section
1700 W. Washington Street, 7th Floor
Phoenix, AZ 85007-2888
E-Mail: notary@azsos.gov
Telephone: (602) 542-6187 or (602) 542-4758
Fax: (602) 542-7386

The Notary Section is located in the State Capitol Executive Tower at 1700 West Washington. Mail is received on the seventh floor; walk-in business is conducted in Suite 103 on the first floor.

In addition, there are many useful resources available at the state's official website, including links to legislation, libraries and public records. You can access the website at www.azsos.gov/notary. ∎

Bureaus of Vital Statistics

Certified Copies. Arizona Notaries are not permitted to make certified copies of birth, death or marriage certificates or of divorce decrees. Persons requesting notarized or certified copies of birth or death certificates should be referred to the appropriate bureau of vital statistics. The following state agencies can provide certified copies of birth and death records for persons who were born or have died in the respective states or territories, as can certain local offices not listed here:

Alabama
Vital Records
Department of Public Health
P.O. Box 5625
Montgomery, AL 36103-5625

Alaska
Bureau of Vital Statistics
Department of Health &
Social Services
5441 Commercial Blvd.
P.O. Box 110675
Juneau, AK 99801

Arizona
Office of Vital Records
Department of Health Services
P.O. Box 3887
Phoenix, AZ 85030-3887

Arkansas
Division of Vital Records
Department of Health
4815 West Markham Street, Slot 44
Little Rock, AR 72205-3867

California
Office of Vital Records
Department of Health Services
P.O. Box 997410, MS: 5103
Sacramento, CA 95899-7410

Colorado
Vital Records Section
Department of Health
4300 Cherry Creek Drive South
Denver, CO 80246-1530

Connecticut
Department of Public Health
State Office of Vital Records
410 Capitol Avenue, MS #11VRS
P.O. Box 340308
Hartford, CT 06134-0308

Delaware
Health Statistics Center
Office of Vital Statistics
Jesse S. Cooper Building
417 Federal Street
Dover, DE 19901

BUREAUS OF VITAL STATISTICS

District of Columbia
Vital Records Division
825 North Capitol Street NE
1st Floor
Washington, DC 20002

Florida
Office of Vital Statistics
1217 Pearl Street
P.O. Box 210
Jacksonville, FL 32231

Georgia
Vital Records
2600 Skyland Drive NE
Atlanta, GA 30319-3640

Hawaii
Vital Statistics Section
State Department of Health
P.O. Box 3378
Honolulu, HI 96801

Idaho
Vital Statistics Unit
450 West State Street, 1st Floor
P.O. Box 83720
Boise, ID 83720-0036

Illinois
Division of Vital Records
Department of Public Health
605 West Jefferson Street
Springfield, IL 62702-5097

Indiana
Vital Records Department
State Department of Health
6 West Washington Street
Indianapolis, IN 46204

Iowa
Department of Public Health
Bureau of Vital Records
Lucas Office Building, 1st Floor
321 East 12th Street
Des Moines, IA 50319-0075

Kansas
Office of Vital Statistics
1000 SW Jackson Street
Suite 120
Topeka, KS 66612-2221

Kentucky
Office of Vital Statistics
Department for Health Services
275 East Main Street, 1E-A
Frankfort, KY 40621-0001

Louisiana
Vital Records Registry
P.O. Box 60630
New Orleans, LA 70160

Maine
Vital Statistics
221 State Street
11 State House Station
Augusta, ME 04333-0011

Maryland
Division of Vital Records
Department of Health
6550 Reisterstown Road
Baltimore, MD 21215

Massachusetts
Registry of Vital Records and
Statistics
150 Mount Vernon Street
1st Floor
Dorchester, MA 02125-3105

Michigan
Vital Records Request
P.O. Box 30721
Lansing, MI 48909

Minnesota
Department of Health
Office of the State Registrar
P.O. Box 64882
St. Paul, MN 55164-0882

Mississippi
Vital Records
P.O. Box 1700
Jackson, MS 39215-1700

Missouri
Department of Health
Bureau of Vital Records
930 Wildwood
P.O. Box 570
Jefferson City, MO 65102-0570

Montana
Office of Vital Statistics
P.O. Box 4210
111 North Sanders, Room 209
Helena, MT 59604

Nebraska
Vital Statistics
Department of Health
301 Centennial Mall South
P.O. Box 95065
Lincoln, NE 68509-5065

Nevada
Office of Vital Records
4150 Technology Way, Suite 104
Carson City, NV 89706

New Hampshire
Department of State
Division of Vital Records
Administration
71 South Fruit Street
Concord, NH 03301-2410

New Jersey
Vital Statistics
Customer Service
P.O. Box 370
Trenton, NJ 08625-0370

New Mexico
Vital Records and Health
Statistics
1105 St. Francis Drive
Santa Fe, NM 87502

New York
State Department of Health
Vital Records Section
Certification Unit
P.O. Box 2602
Albany, NY 12220-2602

New York City
Office of Vital Records
New York City Department of
Health
125 Worth Street, CN4, Room 133
New York, NY 10013

North Carolina
Vital Records
1903 Mail Service Center
Raleigh, NC 27699-1903

North Dakota
Division of Vital Records
600 East Boulevard Avenue
Dept. 301
Bismarck, ND 58505-0200

Ohio
Department of Health
Vital Statistics
P.O. Box 15098
Columbus, OH 43215-0098

Oklahoma
Vital Records Service
State Department of Health
1000 Northeast 10th Street
Oklahoma City, OK 73117

Oregon
Vital Records
P.O. Box 14050
Portland, OR 97293-0050

Pennsylvania
Division of Vital Records
101 South Mercer Street
Room 401
P.O. Box 1528
New Castle, PA 16101

BUREAUS OF VITAL STATISTICS

Rhode Island
Office of Vital Records
Department of Health
3 Capitol Hill Road, Room 101
Providence, RI 02908-5097

South Carolina
Office of Vital Records
South Carolina DHEC
2600 Bull Street
Columbia, SC 29201

South Dakota
Vital Records
207 East Missouri Avenue
Suite #1A
Pierre, SD 57501

Tennessee
Vital Records
Central Services Building
421 5th Avenue North
Nashville, TN 37247

Texas
Bureau of Vital Statistics
Department of Health
P.O. Box 12040
Austin, TX 78711-2040

Utah
Vital Records and Statistics
Cannon Health Building
288 North 1460 West
P.O. Box 141012
Salt Lake City, UT 84114-1012

Vermont
Department of Health
Vital Records Section
108 Cherry Street
P.O. Box 70
Burlington, VT 05402-0070

Virginia
Office of Vital Records
P.O. Box 1000
Richmond, VA 23218-1000

Washington
Department of Health
Center for Health Statistics
P.O. Box 9709
Olympia, WA 98507-9709

West Virginia
Vital Registration Office
350 Capitol Street, Room 165
Charleston, WV 25301-3701

Wisconsin
Vital Records
1 West Wilson Street
P.O. Box 309
Madison, WI 53701-0309

Wyoming
Vital Records Services
Hathaway Building
Cheyenne, WY 82002

American Samoa
Office of Records and Vital Statistics
LBJ Tropical Medical Center
Department of Health Services
American Samoa Government
Pago Pago, AS 96799

Guam
Office of Vital Statistics
Department of Public Health
P.O. Box 2816
Agana, GU, M.I. 96910

Northern Mariana Islands
Bureau of Health Planning
Statistics Office
P.O. Box 500409 CK
Saipan, MP 96950-0409

Panama Canal Zone
Vital Records Section
Passport Services
U.S. Department of State
1111 19th Street NW, Suite 510
Washington, DC 20522-1705

Puerto Rico
Department of Health
Demographic Registry
P.O. Box 11854
Fernández Juncos Station
San Juan, PR 00910

Virgin Islands (St. Croix)
Department of Health
Vital Statistics
Charles Harwood Memorial Hospital
St. Croix, VI 00820

Virgin Islands
(St. Thomas, St. John)
Department of Health
Registrar of Vital Statistics
Knud Hansen Complex
St. Thomas, VI 0080

Hague Convention Nations

The nations listed on the following pages are parties to a treaty called the *Hague Convention Abolishing the Requirement of Legalization [Authentication] for Foreign Public Documents*, hereafter simply called the Hague Convention.

Treaty Simplifies Authentication. A Notary's signature on documents that are sent to these nations may be authenticated (verified as valid for the benefit of the recipient in the foreign nation) through attachment of a single authenticating certificate called an *apostille*. The *apostille* (French for "notation") is the only authenticating certificate necessary. Nations not subscribing to the Hague Convention may require as many as five or six separate authenticating certificates from different governmental agencies, domestic and foreign.

How to Request an *Apostille*. To obtain an *apostille*, anyone may mail the notarized document and the $3 fee to the Secretary of State's office. It is not the Notary's responsibility to obtain an *apostille*; but the responsibility of the party needing authentication. An *apostille* must be specifically requested, and the nation to which the document will be sent must be indicated. A certificate may be obtained by mail or in person from the:

Arizona Secretary of State
Notary Section
1700 W. Washington Street, 7th Floor
Phoenix, AZ 85007-2888

Email: notary@azsos.gov

ARIZONA NOTARY LAW PRIMER

Telephone: (602) 542-6187 or (602) 542-4758

Fax: (602) 542-7386

Hague Convention Nations. The nations listed below participate in the Hague Convention. Footnotes reflect information most likely to be of interest to Notaries acting in the United States and its territories. Please note that some nations listed may not recognize the participation of every other nation listed. To verify recognition between nations, consult the website of the Hague Conference on Private International Law at http://www.hcch.net/index_en.php.

Albania
Andorra[13]
Antigua and Barbuda[13]
Argentina[1]
Armenia[13]
Australia
Austria
Azerbaijan[13]
Bahamas[13]
Barbados[13]
Belarus
Belgium[7]
Belize[13]
Bosnia and Herzegovina[2]
Botswana[13]
Brunei Darussalam[13]
Bulgaria
Colombia[13]
Cook Islands[13]
Croatia[2]
Cyprus
Czech Republic
Denmark[3]
Dominica[13]
Dominican Republic[13]
Ecuador
El Salvador[13]
Estonia
Fiji[13]
Finland
France[4]
Georgia[5]

Germany[7]
Greece
Grenada[13]
Honduras[13]
Hong Kong[6]
Hungary
Iceland
India
Ireland
Israel
Italy
Japan
Kazakhstan[13]
Latvia
Lesotho[13]
Liberia[7,13]
Liechtenstein[13]
Lithuania
Luxembourg
Macao[6]
Macedonia[2]
Malawi[13]
Malta
Marshall Islands[13]
Mauritius[13]
Mexico
Moldova[13]
Monaco
Montenegro[2]
Namibia[13]
Netherlands[8]
New Zealand[9]
Niue[13]
North Korea

Norway
Panama
Poland
Portugal[10]
Romania
Russian Federation
Saint Kitts and Nevis[13]
Saint Lucia[13]
Saint Vincent and the Grenadines[13]
Samoa[13]
San Marino[13]
Sao Tome e Principe[13]
Serbia[2]
Seychelles[13]
Slovakia
Slovenia[2]
South Africa
Spain
Suriname
Swaziland[13]
Sweden
Switzerland
Tonga[13]
Trinidad and Tobago[13]
Turkey
Ukraine
United Kingdom[1,11]
United States[7,12]
Vanuatu[13]
Venezuela

HAGUE CONVENTION NATIONS

<u>Inquiries</u>. Persons having questions about the *Hague Convention Abolishing the Requirement of Legalization for Foreign Public Documents* may address their inquiries to:

Authentication Office
518 23rd Street, NW
State Annex 1
Washington, DC 20037
(202) 647-5002

---

1. Argentina does not recognize the extension of the Convention by the United Kingdom to the Malvinas (Falkland Islands), South Georgia, South Sandwich Islands and the Argentine Antarctic Sector (British Antarctic Territory). See n. 11.
2. The former Socialist Federal Republic of Yugoslavia was a party to the Convention. Only the successor states of Bosnia and Herzegovina, Croatia, the Republic of Macedonia, Montenegro, Serbia and Slovenia have confirmed that the Convention still applies.
3. The participation of Denmark does not extend to Greenland and the Faro Islands.
4. The participation of France is extended to the entire territory of the French Republic, including French Guyana, French Polynesia, Guadeloupe, Martinique, Mayotte, New Caledonia, Reunion, St. Barthelemy, St. Martin, St. Pierre and Miquelon, and Wallis and Futuna.
5. The participation of Georgia does not extend to Abkhazia and South Ossetia.
6. Hong Kong and Macao retained their status as Hague nations after control was returned to China on July 1, 1997 (Hong Kong) and December 20, 1999 (Macao).
7. The participation of New Zealand does not extend to Tokelau.
8. The Convention does not apply between Liberia and the United States, Belgium or Germany.
9. The participation of the Netherlands is extended to Aruba and the Netherlands Antilles.
10. The participation of Portugal is extended to the entire territory of the Republic of Portugal, including the Azores and Madeira.
11. The participation of the United Kingdom of Great Britain and Northern Ireland is extended to Anguilla, Bermuda, British Antarctic Territory, British Virgin Islands, Cayman Islands, Falkland Islands, Gibraltar, Guernsey, Isle of Man, Jersey, Montserrat, St. Helena and Turks and Caicos Islands.
12. The United States includes American Samoa, District of Columbia, Guam, Northern Mariana Islands, Puerto Rico and U.S. Virgin Islands.
13. This nation is not a member of the Hague Conference on Private International Law but is a party to the *Hague Convention Abolishing the Requirement of Legalization for Foreign Public Documents*.

About the NNA

Since 1957, the National Notary Association — a nonprofit educational organization — has served the nation's Notaries Public with a wide variety of instructional programs and services.

As the country's clearinghouse for information on Notary laws, customs and practices, the NNA educates Notaries through publications, seminars, webinars, online training, annual conferences, its website and a Notary Information Service Hotline that offers immediate answers to specific questions about notarization.

The Association is perhaps most widely known as the preeminent source of information for and about Notaries. NNA works include the following:

- *The National Notary*, a magazine for NNA members featuring how-to articles and practical tips on notarizing

- *Notary Bulletin*, an online newsletter that keeps NNA members and customers up to date on developments affecting Notaries, especially new state laws and regulations

- *Sorry, No Can Do!* series, four volumes that help Notaries explain to signers and bosses why some requests for notarizations are improper and cannot be accommodated

- *U.S. Notary Reference Manual*, an invaluable resource for any person relying upon the authenticity and correctness of legal documents

- *Notary Public Practices & Glossary*, a definitive reference book on notarial procedures and widely hailed as the Notary's bible

- *State Notary Law Primers*, short guidebooks that explain a state's Notary statutes in easy-to-understand language

- *The Notary Public Code of Professional Responsibility*, a comprehensive and detailed code of ethical and professional conduct for Notaries

- *The Model Notary Act*, prototype legislation conceived in 1973 and updated in 1984, 2002 and 2010 by an NNA-recruited panel of secretaries of state, legislators and attorneys, and regularly used by state legislatures in revising their Notary laws

- *Notary Law & Practice: Cases & Materials*, the definitive and one-of-a-kind text for teaching Notary law to law students in schools and to attorneys in Minimum Continuing Education Seminars (MCLE), discussing every major judicial decision affecting the Notary's duties

- *Notary Signing Agent Training Course*, a manual covering every aspect of signing agent procedures that prepares candidates for the Notary Signing Agent Certification Examination developed by the NNA

- Public-service pamphlets informing the general public about the function of a Notary, including *What Is A Notary Public?* printed in English and Spanish

In addition, the NNA offers the highest quality professional tools, including official seals and stamps, embossers, recordkeeping journals, thumbprinting devices and notarial certificates.

Though dedicated primarily to educating and assisting Notaries, the NNA devotes part of its resources to helping lawmakers draft effective Notary statutes and to informing the public about the Notary's vital role in modern society. ■

135

Index

A

Acknowledgment..............28, **30–36**
Address change **26–27**, 75–76
Advertising.......................**62–63**, 75
Advice and assistance 20, 61–62, 64–65
Affidavit....................................**38–39**
Affirmation........... 29, **36–39**, 38–40, 44–45, 77–78
Apostille 70–71, 131–132
Application, commission.............4–6, **22–23**, 67, 73
Arizona Administrative Code (*AAC*).............................. *118–123*
  R2-12-1101 ....*118*
  R2-12-1102 ....*118*
  R2-12-1103 .... *119–120*
  R2-12-1201 .... *119–120*
  R2-12-1202 ....*120*
  R2-12-1203 .... *121–122*
  R2-12-1204 ....*121*
  R2-12-1205 ....*122*
  R2-12-1206 ....*122*
  R2-12-1207 ....*123*
  R2-12-1208 ....*123*
  R2-12-1209 ....*123*
Arizona Revised Statutes (*ARS*) *86–116*
  Section 10-2082.......................*107*
  Section 12-284.........................*107*
  Section 14-5501............... *108–110*
  Section 16-828.........................*109*
  Section 26-160.........................*110*
  Section 33-501................ *110–111*
  Section 33-502.........................*110*
  Section 33-503..........................*111*
  Section 33-504..........................*111*
  Section 33-505..........................*111*
  Section 33-506................ *112–113*
  Section 33-507.........................*113*
  Section 33-508.........................*113*
  Section 33-511.........................*113*
  Section 33-512.........................*113*
  Section 33-513.........................*113*
  Section 36-2152....................... 114
  Section 38-233................ *114–115*
  Section 38-291................ *115–116*
  Section 38-294.........................*115*
  Section 38-412.........................*116*
  Section 38-413.........................*116*
  Section 38-423................ *116–117*
  Section 39-122.........................*116*
  Section 39-161.........................*117*
  Section 41-126................ *117–118*
  Section 41-311...................*86–87*
  Section 41-312...................*88–89*
  Section 41-313...................*89–90*
  Section 41-314...........................*90*
  Section 41-315...........................*90*
  Section 41-316...........................*90*
  Section 41-317...........................*90*
  Section 41-318...........................*91*
  Section 41-319...................*91–92*

INDEX

Section 41-320............................*92*
Section 41-321......................*92–93*
Section 41-322............................*93*
Section 41-323......................*93–94*
Section 41-324............................*94*
Section 41-325............................*94*
Section 41-326............................*94*
Section 41-327............................*94*
Section 41-328............................*95*
Section 41-329............................*95*
Section 41-330......................*95–96*
Section 41-331......................*96, 97*
Section 41-351......................*97–99*
Section 41-352....................*99–100*
Section 41-353....................*99–100*
Section 41-354..........................*101*
Section 41-355..................*101–102*
Section 41-356..........................*102*
Section 41-357..........................*102*
Section 41-358..........................*102*
Section 41-359..................*103–104*
Section 41-360..........................*103*
Section 41-361..................*103–104*
Section 41-362..........................*104*
Section 41-363..........................*104*
Section 41-364..................*105–106*
Section 41-365..........................*105*
Section 41-366..........................*105*
Section 41-367..........................*106*
Section 41-368..................*106–107*
Section 41-369..........................*107*
Section 41-370..................*107–108*
Section 42-11152......................*117*
Attorney General Opinions.........*124*
    Opinion I97-011 (R97-033)....*124*
    Opinion I97-015 (R97-040)....*124*
Authentication... 66, **69–71**, 131–133
Authorized acts............................ **28**
Awareness................................... 17

B

Beneficial interest........................ 14
Birth certificate....... 13, 29, 35, 126

Blank spaces......... 16, 29, 65, 74, 76
Bond.......................5, **23–24**, 68, 73
Bureaus of Vital Statistics....... 13, 35, **126–130**

C

Certificate
    Authenticating.................... **70–71**
    Commission 6, **25**, 73
    Naturalization......................65, 77
    Notarial....8, 18–20, 34–35, **50–53**, 63, 74, 76
Certified copies..........13, **35–37**, 48
Notarial records, of............. 48–49
Change of name or address.. **26–27**, 75–76
Civil penalty....26, 49, 55, 69, **72–77**
Commission certificate 6, **25**, 73
Copy certification 13, **35–37**
Credible person..... 10–11, 16, 37–38, **44–46**
Criminal penalty ...36, 38, 53, **72–77**

D

Date
    Commission expiration ...7, 26–27, 51, 55, 67–68
    Document 16
    Notarization 18, 46, 49, 51, 68
Death certificate.............. 29, 35, 126
Death of Notary.................... **28–29**
Deposition 30, **39**

E

Electronic
    Certificate..................... *121–123*
    Notarizations..................... **67–71**
Notary................. 21, 23, 26, 67–69
Embosser..7
Employment
    Termination of............... 28, 49–50
Errors and omissions insurance...... 9, **78–79**

Page numbers listed in **bold** indicate where the most complete information on a subject can be found. *Italics* indicate pages where the statutes and state-published information pertaining to a subject are located.

137

F

False Certificate..................... **53**
Family members 14, 61
Fees
  Application................ 5–6, **23**, 73
  Authentication.................. 71, 131
  Notarial .. 46, **56–58**, 61, 66, 69, 75
  Travel **58**
Felony 3, 22, 53, 58, 63, **74–76**
Foreign Language
  Documents......... 13, 51, 59, 63–64
  Speakers..................... 31, 39, 64

H

Hague Convention.. 70–71, **131–133**

I

Identification................ 10–11, 16–17,
  41–47, 60
Identification documents......... 16–17,
  42–44
Immigration **62–64**
Incomplete
  Certificate............................. 50, 77
  Document 16, 29, 40, 65, 76

J

Journal of notarial acts 8–9, 18,
  27–28, **45–49**, 69, 75, 77
Jurat 8, 14, 16, 29, **38–40**, 65, 76
Jurisdiction.................................. **25**

L

Language requirement 3
Laws pertaining to Notaries
  Public 86–122
Lawsuit 62, 73
Liability..................... **72–73**, 78–79
Locus sigilli............................. **51**, 55
Loose certificate........... 11–12, 13, 18,
  19–20, **52–53**, 55

M

Material benefit.................. 60–61, 76
Military-officer notarizations ... 65–66
Minors 60
Misconduct...... 36, 40, 53, 69, **71–77**
Misdemeanor 72

N

Name change..............**26**, 75–76
National Notary
  Association...................... 134–135
Notarial acts **28–44**, 78–79
Notary laws explained 21–82

O

Oath 29, **36–41**, 44–45, 77–78
Oath of office.................**25–26**, 36
Office of the Arizona Secretary
  of State 125

P

Penalties....49, 53, 55, 65, 69, **71–78**
Personal appearance ... 13–14, 15–16,
  69–70
Personal knowledge of
  identity 10–11, 16–17, **41**
Photocopies 12, **35–37**
Photographs................................... 11
Practices and procedures 41–72
Prohibited acts 73–77
Proof of execution by subscribing
  witness 30–31
Protests... 40
Public records 13, 29, 30, 35, 45,
  48–49, 53, 126

Q

Qualifications................. 3–4, **22**, 67

R

Reappointment 4, 23, 27
Reasonable care..................... 15, **78**
Refusal of services... 12–13, 47, 58–59
Relatives 14, 61
Representative capacity.....31–32, 41,
  47
Residency requirement..3, 22, 26, 68
Resignation 27, 49, 56
Revocation of commission **71–76**

S

Satisfactory evidence.............. **41–44**
Scilicet 50
Seal............. 7, 11, 19, 27, 51, **54–56**,
  67–68, 74–77

INDEX

Secretary of State 3–4, 21–23, 125
Services, notarial 12, 56–58
Signature
    Comparing 17
    Mark, by 29, **59–60**
    Notary, of ... 11, 19, 26, 29, **51–53**,
        60–61, 66, 67, 70, 76
    Stamp 6–8, 51, **54–56**
Statement of particulars 50
Steps to proper notarization ... 15–20

T
Term of office 26
Testimonium clause 51–52
Thumbprint 8, 18, 44, **47**
Tools of the trade 7–10
Training course **4**, **23**, 27
Translator's declaration 65

U
Unauthorized
    Acts 29–30
    Practice of law **61–62**, 64–65
    Understanding 17, 61

V
Venue 8, 19, 39–40, **50**
Vital records 13, 126

W
Willingness 17
Wills 10, **62**
Witness 11, 29–31, 39, **44–46**,
        59–60

Page numbers listed in **bold** indicate where the most complete information on a subject can be found. *Italics* indicate pages where the statutes and state-published information pertaining to a subject are located.

PROTECTION NOW AND AFTER YOUR COMMISSION ENDS.

If an unintentional mistake is made, or a false claim is filed against you, it could cost you thousands of dollars to defend yourself in a lawsuit. With Errors & Omissions Insurance from the NNA, you don't have to worry. Various limits of liability are available to meet your individual needs, and your policy:

- Covers the claim, legal defense fees, and court costs up to your policy's limit
- Doesn't require repayment of claims by the Notary
- Doesn't require a deductible payment

Purchase peace of mind now by visiting NationalNotary.org/Insurance or calling 1-888-896-6827

BONDS AND E&O POLICIES UNDERWRITTEN BY MERCHANTS BONDING COMPANY (MUTUAL), DES MOINES, IOWA. PENNSYLVANIA BONDS AND E&O POLICIES UNDERWRITTEN BY MERCHANTS NATIONAL BONDING, INC. (A SUBSIDIARY OF MERCHANTS BONDING COMPANY (MUTUAL). AGENT FOR ALL BONDS AND E&O POLICIES IS NNA INSURANCE SERVICES, INC. COMMISSION NUMBER AND COMMISSION EFFECTIVE AND EXPIRATION DATES REQUIRED FOR E&O POLICY ACTIVATION. THE COVERAGE PROVIDED BY ANY POLICY ISSUED SHALL BE DETERMINED IN ACCORDANCE WITH THE TERMS AND CONDITIONS OF THE POLICY ISSUED, ANY CONTRARY REPRESENTATIONS HEREIN NOTWITHSTANDING. NNA BENEFITS AND OTHER OFFERINGS COULD CHANGE WITHOUT NOTICE. CALL 1-800-US NOTARY (1-800-876-6827) FOR PRICING AND ORDER INFORMATION.

Source Code
A46151

© 2012 National Notary Association

NOTES